
WOMEN'S ISSUES: GLOBAL TRENDS

Native Women in the Americas

Women in North America's Religious World

Women in the African World

Women in the Hispanic World

Women in the Japanese World

Women in the Mediterranean World

Women in the Modern Arab World

Women in the World of China

Women in the World of Eastern Europe

Women in the World of India

Women in the World of Russia

Women in the World of Southeast Asia

WOMEN'S ISSUES:
GLOBAL TRENDS

WOMEN IN THE MEDITERRANEAN WORLD

BY
AUTUMN LIBAL

Mason Crest Publishers
Philadelphia

Mason Crest Publishers Inc.
370 Reed Road
Broomall, Pennsylvania 19008
(866) MCP-BOOK (toll free)
www.masoncrest.com

13 12 11 10 09 08 07 06 10 9 8 7 6 5 4 3 2

ISBN 1-59084-868-3
ISBN 1-59084-856-X (series)

Library of Congress Cataloging-in-Publication Data

Libal, Autumn.
Women in the Mediterranean world / by Autumn Libal.
p. cm. — (Women's issues, global trends)
Includes bibliographical references and index.
ISBN 1-59084-860-8
1. Women—Mediterranean Region—Social conditions. 2. Women—Mediterranean Region—History. 3. Women—Mediterranean Region—Biography. I. Title. II. Series.
HQ1725.7.L53 2005
305.42'09182'2—dc22
2004010070

Interior design by Michelle Bouch and MK Bassett-Harvey.
Illustrations by Michelle Bouch.
Produced by Harding House Publishing Service, Inc.
www.hardinghousepages.com
Cover design by Benjamin Stewart.
Printed in India.

CONTENTS

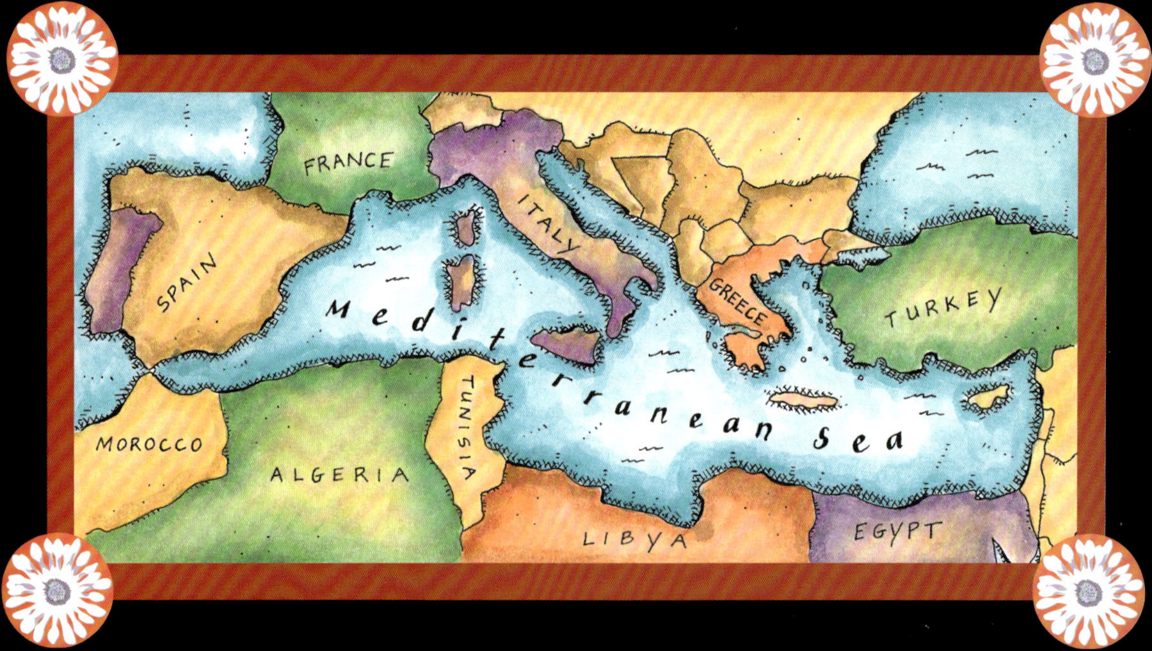

FRANCE
SPAIN
ITALY
GREECE
TURKEY
Mediterranean Sea
MOROCCO
ALGERIA
TUNISIA
LIBYA
EGYPT

INTRODUCTION

by Mary Jo Dudley

The last thirty years have been a time of great progress for women around the world. In some countries, especially where women have more access to education and work opportunities, the relationships between women and men have changed radically. The boundaries between men's roles and women's roles have been crossed, and women are enjoying many experiences that were denied them in past centuries.

But there is still much to be done. On the global stage, women are increasingly the ones who suffer most from poverty. At the same time that they produce 75 to 90 percent of the world's food crops, they are also responsible for taking care of their households. According to the United Nations, in no country in the world do men come anywhere near to spending as much time on housework as women do. This means that women's job opportunities are often extremely limited, contributing to the "feminization of poverty."

In fact, two out of every three poor adults are women. According to the Decade of Women, "Women do two-thirds of the world's work, receive 10 percent of the world's income, and own one percent of the means of production." Women often have no choice but to take jobs that lack long-term security or adequate pay; many women work in dangerous working conditions or in unprotected home-based industries. This series clearly illustrates how historic events and contemporary trends (such as war, conflicts, and migration) have also contributed to women's loss of property and diminished access to resources.

A recent report from Human Rights Watch indicates that many countries continue to deny women basic legal protections. Amnesty International points out, "Governments are not living up to their promises under the Women's Convention to protect women from discrimination and violence such as rape and female genital mutilation." Many nations—including the United States—have not ratified the United Nations' Women's Treaty.

During times of armed conflict, especially under policies of ethnic cleansing, women are particularly at risk. Murder, torture, systematic rape, forced pregnancy and forced abortions are all too common human rights violations endured by women around the world. This series presents the experience of women in Vietnam, Cambodia, the Middle East, and other war torn regions.

In the political arena, equality between men and women has still not been achieved. Around the world, women are underrepresented in their local and national governments; on average, women represent only 10 percent of all legislators worldwide. This series provides excellent examples of key female leaders who have promoted women's rights and occupied unique leadership positions, despite historical contexts that would normally have shut them out from political and social prominence.

The Fourth World Conference on Women called upon the international community to take action in the following areas of concern:

- the persistent and increasing burden of poverty on women
- inequalities and inadequacies in access to education and training
- inequalities and inadequacies in access to health care and related services
- violence against women

- the effects of armed or other kinds of conflict on women
- inequality in economic structures and policies, in all forms of productive processes, and in access to resources
- insufficient mechanisms at all levels to promote the advancement of women
- lack of protection of women's human rights
- stereotyping of women and inequality in women's participation in all community systems, especially the media
- gender inequalities in the management of natural resources and the safeguarding of the environment
- persistent discrimination against and violation of the rights of female children

The Conference's mission statement includes these sentences: "Equality between women and men is a matter of human rights and a condition for social justice and is also a necessary and fundamental prerequisite for equality, development and peace . . . equality between women and men is a condition . . . for society to meet the challenges of the twenty-first century." This series provides examples of how women have risen above adversity, despite their disadvantaged social, economic, and political positions.

Each book in WOMEN'S ISSUES: GLOBAL TRENDS takes a look at women's lives in a different key region or culture, revealing the history, contributions, triumphs, and challenges of women around the world. Women play key roles in shaping families, spirituality, and societies. By interweaving historic backdrops with the modern-day evolving role of women in the home and in society at large, this series presents the important part women play as cultural communicators. Protection of women's rights is an integral part of universal human rights, peace, and economic security. As a result, readers who gain understanding of women's lives around the world will have deeper insight into the current condition of global interactions.

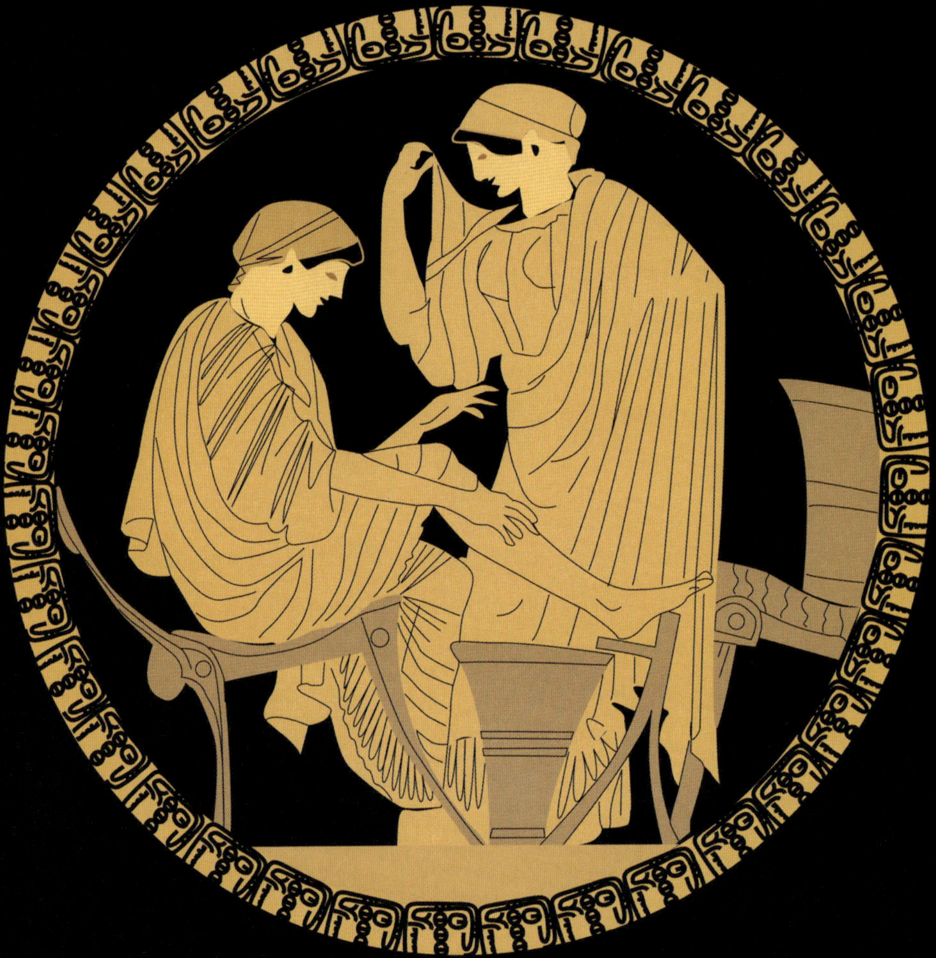

"SENTENCES THAT BEGIN WITH 'ALL WOMEN'
ARE NEVER, NEVER TRUE."
—MARGARET CULKIN BANNING

1

AN INTRODUCTION TO THE MEDITERRANEAN REGION

Sunny beaches, ancient ruins, juicy olives, and exotic marketplaces—these are the things many people think of when they hear the word "Mediterranean." The Mediterranean Sea is a huge, inland body of salt water, and Europe, Africa, and Asia all meet on its shores. Among other things, the Mediterranean is famous for its climate, foods, arts, and cultures.

Each of the lovely things mentioned above could be found in some part of this region, but they do not form a complete picture of this area. Other images, some of them troubling, like civil wars, UN Peacekeepers, and suicide bombings, could also be associated with this vast region.

If you were to walk around the entire Mediterranean Sea, you would travel more than 16,000 miles (approximately 26,000 kilometers). That's like walking across the United States more than five times! On this amazing trip, you could visit twenty-one Mediterranean countries, and you would soon learn that these lands are incredibly diverse. Therefore, when discussing women's lives in the Mediterranean, we must be careful not to generalize too much or resort to ***stereotypes***. Instead, we must examine the whole region, learning about the sim-

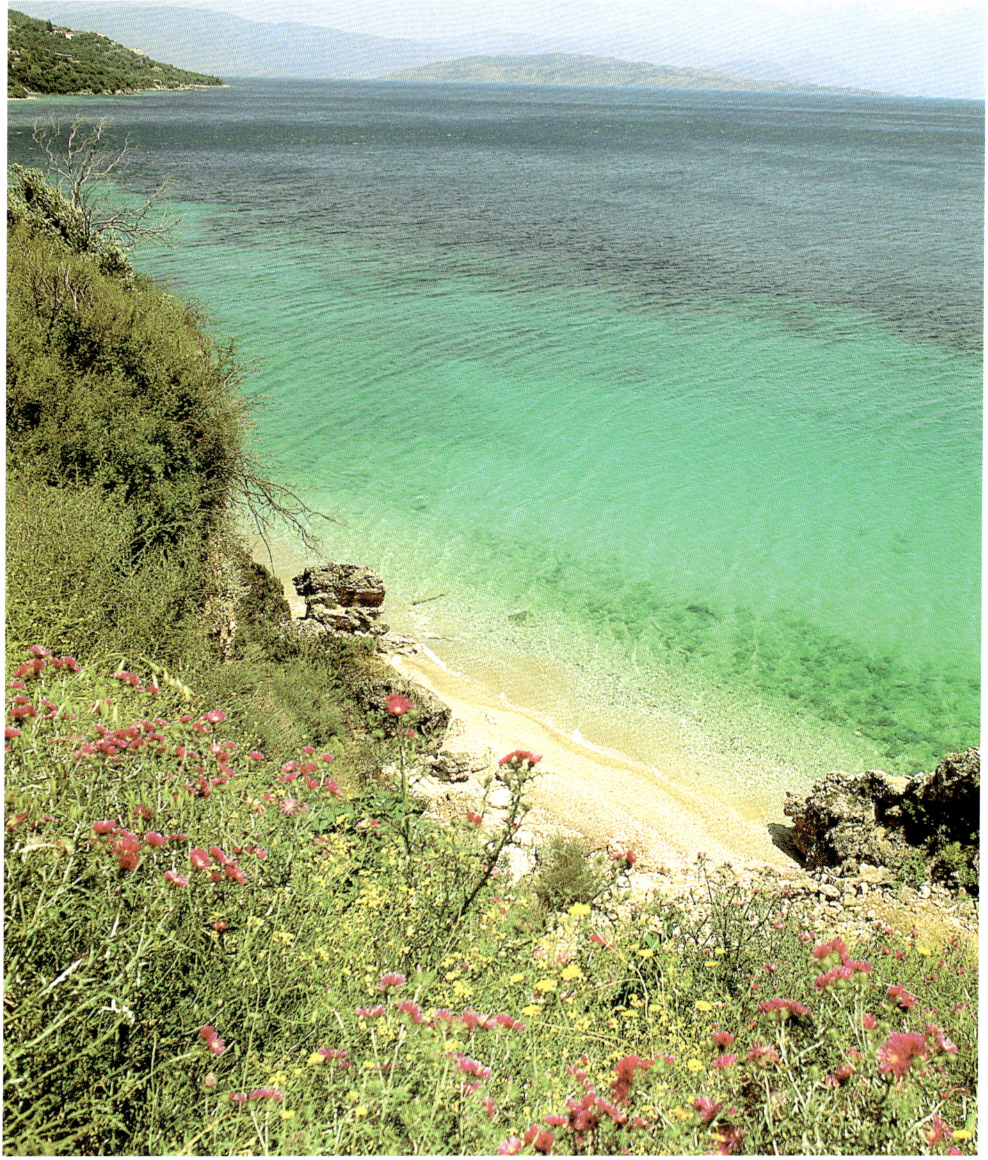

The Mediterranean Sea.

ilarities and differences in women's lives. Before we can learn more about Mediterranean women's experiences, however, we must first know a little bit about the countries in which these women live.

Understanding what life is like in places far from your home can be difficult. Sometimes visiting a place in person is the only way to understand what life is really like there. If you are like most people, however, you probably can't afford to go traveling all over the world, but you still might want to know about life in other countries. Certain information, like quality of life indicators—measurements of things like household wealth, health, and education—can help us understand what life is like in a region even if we can't visit that region in person.

Per capita Gross Domestic Product (GDP) is a tool for measuring a region's wealth. Per capita GDP is the total value of all goods and services produced within a country in a given period of time (this is the GDP) divided by the country's population. The resulting number tells us how much money the country is producing for each person. Countries with high per capita GDPs usually have a higher standard of living than those with low per capita GDPs. However, per capita GDP can be misleading because wealth is rarely distributed evenly throughout a population. In some countries, a small number of people have the majority of the country's wealth while a large number of people have little wealth or even live in poverty. For example, at more than $36,000, the United States has the highest per capita GDP in the world. But the Central Intelligence Agency's (CIA's) *The World Factbook* states, "Since 1975, practically all the gains in household income have gone to the top 20% of households." Furthermore, the top ten percent of the population controls more than 30 percent of the United States' wealth, while the bottom ten percent controls less than two percent of the wealth. In this case, the average household is less prosperous than the per capita GDP implies. Since per capita GDP is not a reliable indicator of actual household wealth, we need to combine it with other indicators to understand what real people's lives are like in a country.

Some other indicators that are important for measuring quality of life are unemployment, life expectancy, ***literacy***, and ***infant mortality*** rates. Low unemployment rates are a sign of a healthy economy. High life expectancy and low infant mortality rates suggest that a population is in good health and has access to adequate medical care. High literacy rates tell us that a country has a strong educational system. Using statistics like these, we can learn a lot about the quality of life in different areas of the Mediterranean.

Eleven countries make up Mediterranean Europe. They are Spain, France, Monaco, Italy, Slovenia, Croatia, Bosnia and Herzegovina, Serbia and Montenegro, Albania, Greece, and the island-country of Malta. According to information collected by the United Nations and the CIA, the European countries are generally the most prosperous and have the highest quality of life in the Mediterranean region. France, for example, has one of the largest economies in the ***Western*** industrialized world and is second only to the United States in agricultural production. Monaco, at approximately $27,000, has the highest annual per capita GDP in the Mediterranean.

Spain, France, Monaco, Italy, Malta, and Greece all have higher life expectancy rates than the United States. These countries also have low infant mortality rates and nearly universal literacy for people under age twenty-four (all information on life expectancy, infant mortality, and literacy rates is based on the United Nations' estimates for 2005 through 2010). Furthermore, although their unemployment rates are rather high by North American standards, they are still low for the Mediterranean region. All these countries have majority-urban populations (meaning that more people live in cities and densely populated areas than live in small towns, villages, and rural areas), and urban areas have well-established ***infrastructure*** for supporting these populations.

Monaco is the second smallest country in the world. With an entire area of only .75 square miles (1.95 square kilometers) and a population of approximately 32,000 people, the entire country is just one small city! Moving at a leisurely pace, you could easily walk from one end of the country to another in a single afternoon. The only smaller country in the world is the Holy See (better known as the Vatican City) in Italy.

Not all of Mediterranean Europe, however, is prosperous. The Balkan States of Croatia, Bosnia and Herzegovina, Serbia and Montenegro, and Albania all face significant difficulties. So what makes these countries different from the rest of Europe? That's a very complicated question, but many of their difficulties arise from their location, ***ethnic*** tensions, and recent communist past.

THE BALKAN STATES

For thousands of years, the Mediterranean Sea has been important for trading and commerce. The Balkans, sandwiched between the sea's western and eastern shores, was a ***coveted*** region. For most of recorded history, foreign powers attempted to control Balkan lands and trade routes. Over time, the Roman, Byzantine, Ottoman, and Austrian-Hungarian Empires were among those who dominated the region. At the dawn of the twentieth century, events in this region sparked World War I—one of the bloodiest conflicts the world has ever seen.

After World War II, much of the region joined Yugoslavia, a federation of communist states. Many different ethnic groups were part of Yugoslavia, and no one group wanted to be ruled by another. The Communist Party of Yugoslavia

In the United States, communism has a bad name and is associated with brutality, poverty, and "evil" regimes. The basic idea of communism, however, was to develop a society where everyone was equal. All land, property, and wealth would be held in common. Everyone would contribute equally to the community, and everyone would partake equally in the fruits of the community's work. In this system, no one in the society would become fabulously rich, but nobody would be terribly poor either. The communist system was especially attractive to people who had spent years under the domination of others.

kept a tight reign on all the regions, and ethnic tensions were kept in check by a leadership willing to crush any hint of unrest with violence. In this oppressive environment, tensions festered. To make matters worse, markets were not able to develop freely as they did elsewhere in Europe, and resources were strained by the need to produce enough food and goods for the populations. All the wealth generated within these states was controlled (and often terribly mismanaged) by the communist party.

Throughout the early 1990s, the republics declared independence from Yugoslavia. Long-suppressed tensions finally erupted causing nearly a decade of wars, political strife, and conflicts between ethnic groups. ***Ethnic cleansing*** occurred in many different areas, and floods of refugees ***destabilized*** some regions. War took its toll on everything from the economy, to education, to health care.

To date, the only country that has emerged from Yugoslavia and achieved relative economic success and high quality of life is Slovenia. Throughout communist rule, Slovenia was the most prosperous Yugoslav republic, which put it a step ahead of the other republics when it declared independence in 1990. Also unlike the other republics, Slovenia's independence was achieved with very little bloodshed—the war they were forced to fight with Yugoslavia lasted only ten days. Today, at $18,000, Slovenia's per capita GDP is nearly on par with Greece (Greece is also considered part of the Balkans, but it was never part of Yugoslavia). Unemployment rates are a concern, but at 11 percent Slovenia's unemployment is still slightly lower than Spain's. Just like the other European states, Slovenia has nearly universal literacy and a very low infant mortality rate. Its life expectancy is roughly the same as that in the United States.

All the other former-Yugoslav states are experiencing significant difficulties. Croatia's unemployment rate is more than 20 percent. Bosnia and Herzegovina's per capita GDP is less than $2,000, and its unemployment rate is 40 percent. Though fairing somewhat better than Bosnia and Herzegovina, Serbia and Montenegro also has a very low per capita GDP and high unemployment.

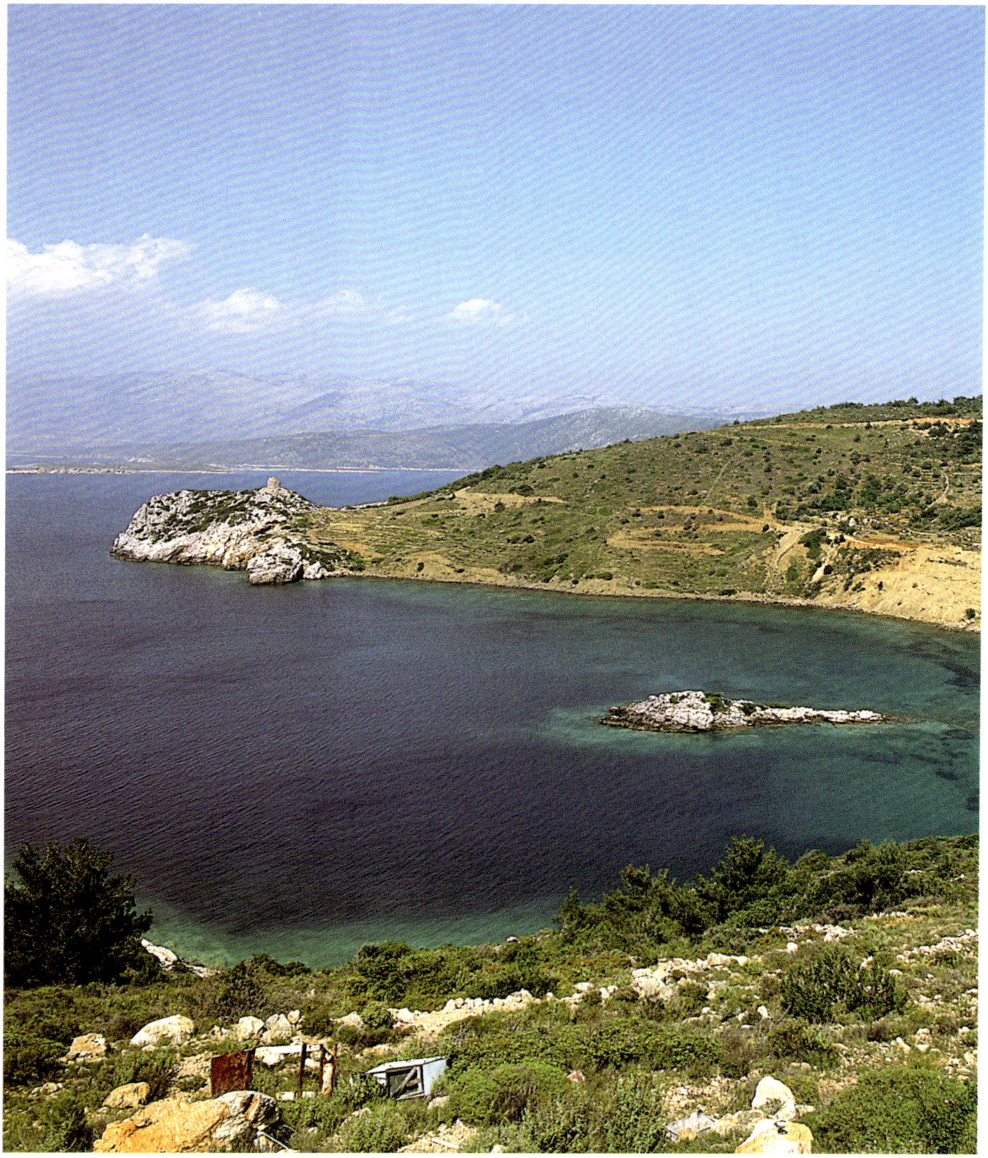

Many countries border the Mediterranean.

These states have large rural populations and rely more on agriculture and industry than their more prosperous European counterparts.

Albania was not part of Yugoslavia, but it struggles with many of the same issues as the other Balkan States. It too suffered under an oppressive communist regime and attempted to adopt democracy in the 1990s. Widespread corruption in the government and the economy has made democracy a difficult road. Today, its per capita GDP is higher than that of neighboring Serbia and Montenegro, but at over twenty-two deaths per one thousand births, their infant mortality rate is the highest in Mediterranean Europe. Albania's literacy rates are somewhat lower than the rest of Europe. The majority of the population lives in rural areas, and agriculture makes up the largest portion of the economy.

Mediterranean Asia

Five countries make up Mediterranean Asia. They are Turkey, Lebanon, Syria, Israel, and the island-country of Cyprus. If we rely on the same measurements and indicators, we can conclude that only one country in Mediterranean Asia has roughly the same quality of life as the prosperous Mediterranean European countries. This country is Israel, which has a per capita income of approximately $19,000 (the same as Greece), a service based-economy with a large high-tech sector, nearly universal literacy for people under twenty-four, a life expectancy higher than that in the United States, and a low infant-mortality rate.

Israel, however, is not without its problems. On almost any given day, Israel is likely to be in the news for the conflicts between its Jewish and Arab populations. The basic reasons for these conflicts are land disputes. The Arab people had controlled this region since 634 C.E. In the nineteenth century, ***colonial*** European influence increased in the area. Jewish people, many of whom faced persecution in Europe, began immigrating to the area in the late nineteenth century, displacing many of the Arab people who already lived there. When the state of Israel was created in 1948, the surrounding countries of Lebanon, Syria, Jordan, and Egypt all invaded. Wars and skirmishes, punctuated by treaties, cease-fires, and brief periods of peace, have continued ever since. Today's violence, characterized by Israeli military occupations of ***Palestinian*** territories and Palestinian suicide bombings in Israel, began in 2000.

Cyprus is also a country divided, and these divisions have a significant impact on quality of life. The population of northern Cyprus is Turkish while the population of southern Cyprus is Greek. The north has actually declared itself the Turkish Republic of Northern Cyprus, but no country except Turkey recognizes the area's independence. Cyprus's political split affects its economy. In the Greek area, annual per capita GDP is approximately $15,000, and there is a large service sector. In the Turkish area, however, the annual per capita GDP is approximately $7,000, and there is a larger focus on agriculture and industry. According to our other indicators, however, Cyprus is doing quite well. The country's unemployment is the lowest of any Mediterranean country. Like Israel and many of the European countries, Cyprus has nearly universal literacy for people under age twenty-four, boasts a life expectancy higher than that in the United States, and has low infant mortality. Seventy percent of Cyprus's population lives in urban areas.

The remaining states in Mediterranean Asia—Turkey, Lebanon, and Syria—face significant difficulties in each of our measured areas. Their annual per capita GDPs are approximately $7,000, $5,200, and $3,200, respectively. About one in every five people of working age in Lebanon and Syria are unemployed. Though these countries have made great strides in improving access to education, the number of illiterate people remains quite high. Infant mortality rates are also troublingly high in all three countries, with Turkey having the highest rate of approximately thirty-four deaths in every one thousand births.

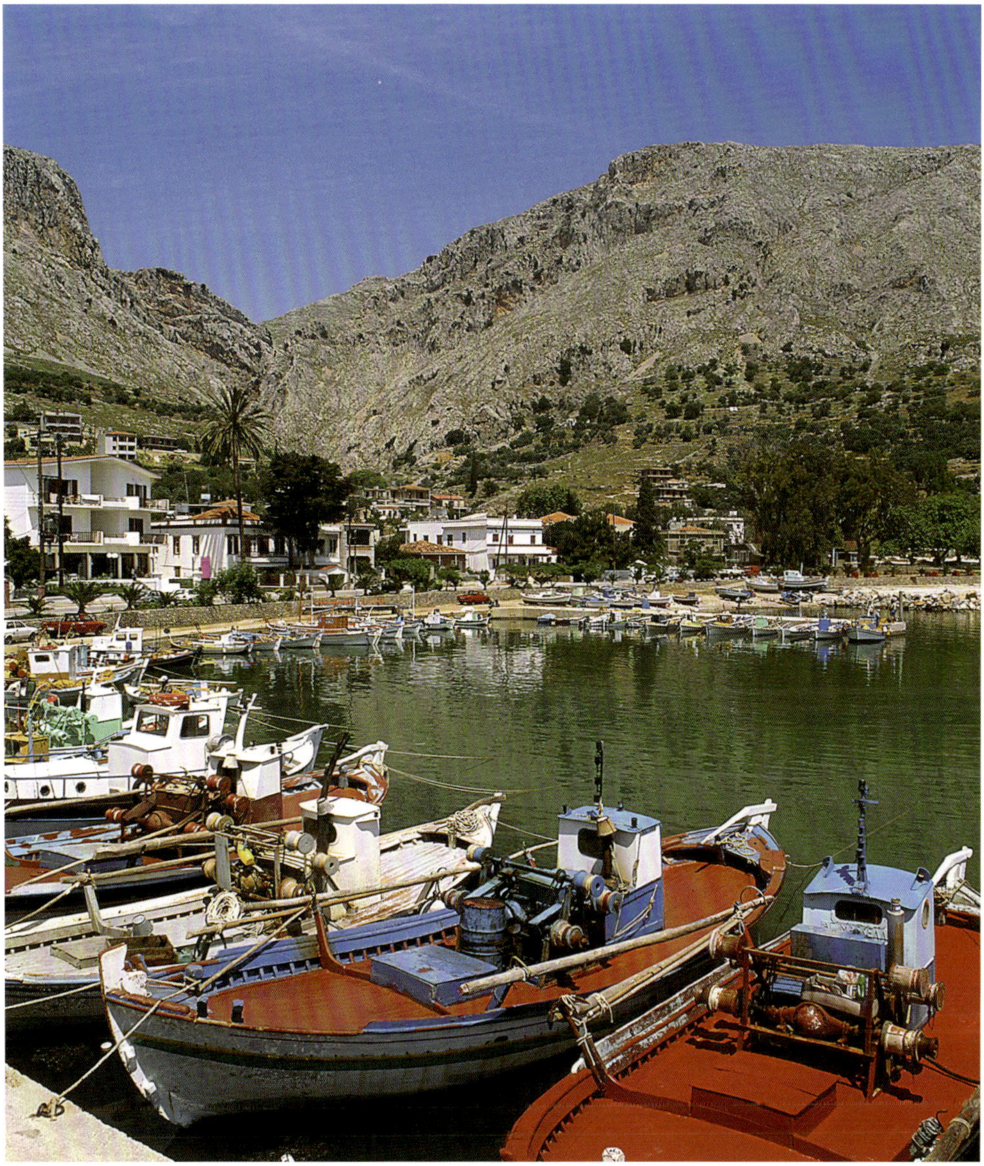

Fishing is a big industry in the Mediterranean region.

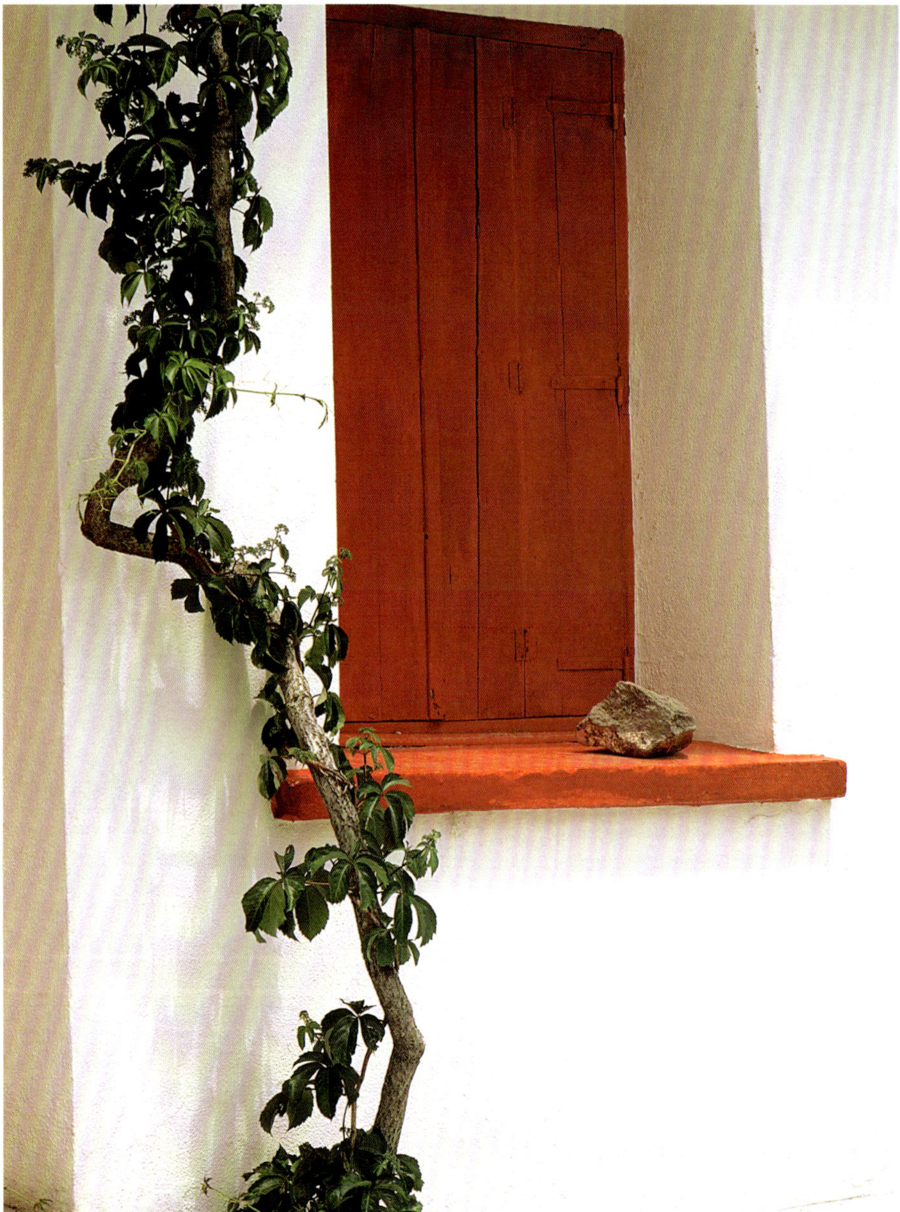

The majority of the population lives in urban areas, but cities do not always have the infrastructure to support their populations. In some areas, there are not enough clean water sources, sewage facilities, electricity and telephone lines, or roads to service the rapid influx of people from rural to urban areas. In the last fifteen years, Lebanon has had to work particularly hard to rebuild such services as much of their infrastructure was destroyed in a civil war that lasted from 1975 until 1991.

Mediterranean North Africa

There are five North African countries bordering the Mediterranean Sea: Egypt, Libya, Tunisia, Algeria, and Morocco. Beginning in the nineteenth and ending in the mid-twentieth century, Great Britain, France, Italy, and Spain controlled these North African lands. During the colonial era, European countries invaded and dominated lands around the world, using their citizens as laborers and extracting the countries' natural resources. Development in colonies was designed to benefit the colonizers while keeping the colonized people oppressed. Governments were run by the colonial powers, and all the wealth generated by the colonies' resources went to foreign hands rather than benefiting the native people. In the mid-twentieth century, colonial rule ended in many areas, but this did not mean North Africa's troubles were over. The colonial powers wiped their hands clean of the many problems—like poverty, political instability, environmental ***degradation***, and lack of education—that they had created. At the same time, having denied the colonized people any chance to participate meaningfully in government, they left the nations poorly equipped to meet the challenges of independence. Keeping this in mind, it's easy to understand why the North African nations face so many complicated challenges today.

When stepping from Mediterranean Asia to Mediterranean North Africa, the first country we enter is Egypt. Egyptian society has existed for more than five thousand years! It had one of the great ancient civilizations, but since about 500 B.C.E. Egypt has been controlled by foreign empires. The Persian, Greek, Roman, and Ottoman empires are among those who seized Egypt at different times. Great Britain occupied Egypt in the colonial period. Egypt gained independence in 1922, but wanting to control Egypt's valuable ***Suez Canal***, Great Britain maintained a political and military presence for many years. Egypt also experienced many years of tension, clashes, and war with Israel. Since 1977, however, Egypt has been committed to maintaining peaceful relations with Israel, making the country's policies toward Israel unique in the Arab world.

Today, as in times past, the majority of Egypt's population lives along the Nile River, making the Nile delta one of the most densely populated parts of the world. This creates incredible difficulties for the country. With over seventy-million people inhabiting its banks, the Nile's resources are over-taxed, and pollution from sewage, industry, and agricultural runoff chokes its waters. The country also struggles with a low per capita GDP of $3,700, low life expectancy, high infant mortality, and low literacy rates. Agriculture is extremely important to Egypt's people and economy. About one out of every three laborers works in agriculture, and in some places ***urbanization*** and environmental degradation seriously threaten farmland.

Libya, whose official name is Great Socialist People's Libyan Arab Jamahiriya, was controlled by Italy in the colonial period. Today, it has the highest per capita GDP (approximately $7,600) in Mediterranean North Africa. Libya's GDP, however, is somewhat deceiving. Most of the country's income comes from oil revenues, which are controlled by the government and do not benefit the lower economic classes. Libya is putting some of its wealth to good use. It has the highest literacy rates, the lowest infant mortality rates, and is tied with Tunisia for the highest life expectancy rates of the North African countries. However, in recent decades Libya has used its wealth for destructive

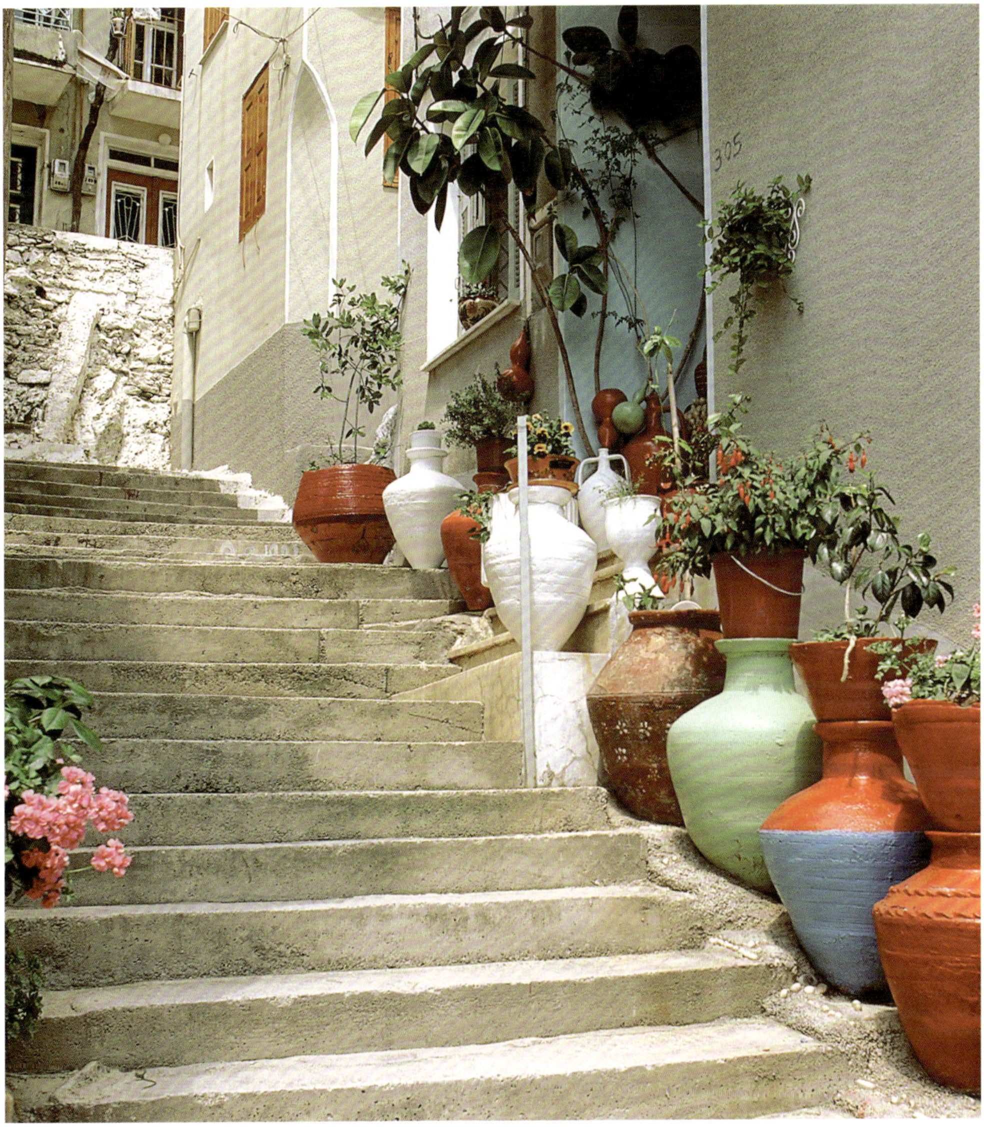

The Mediterranean region is one of bright colors, rich culture—and great problems as well.

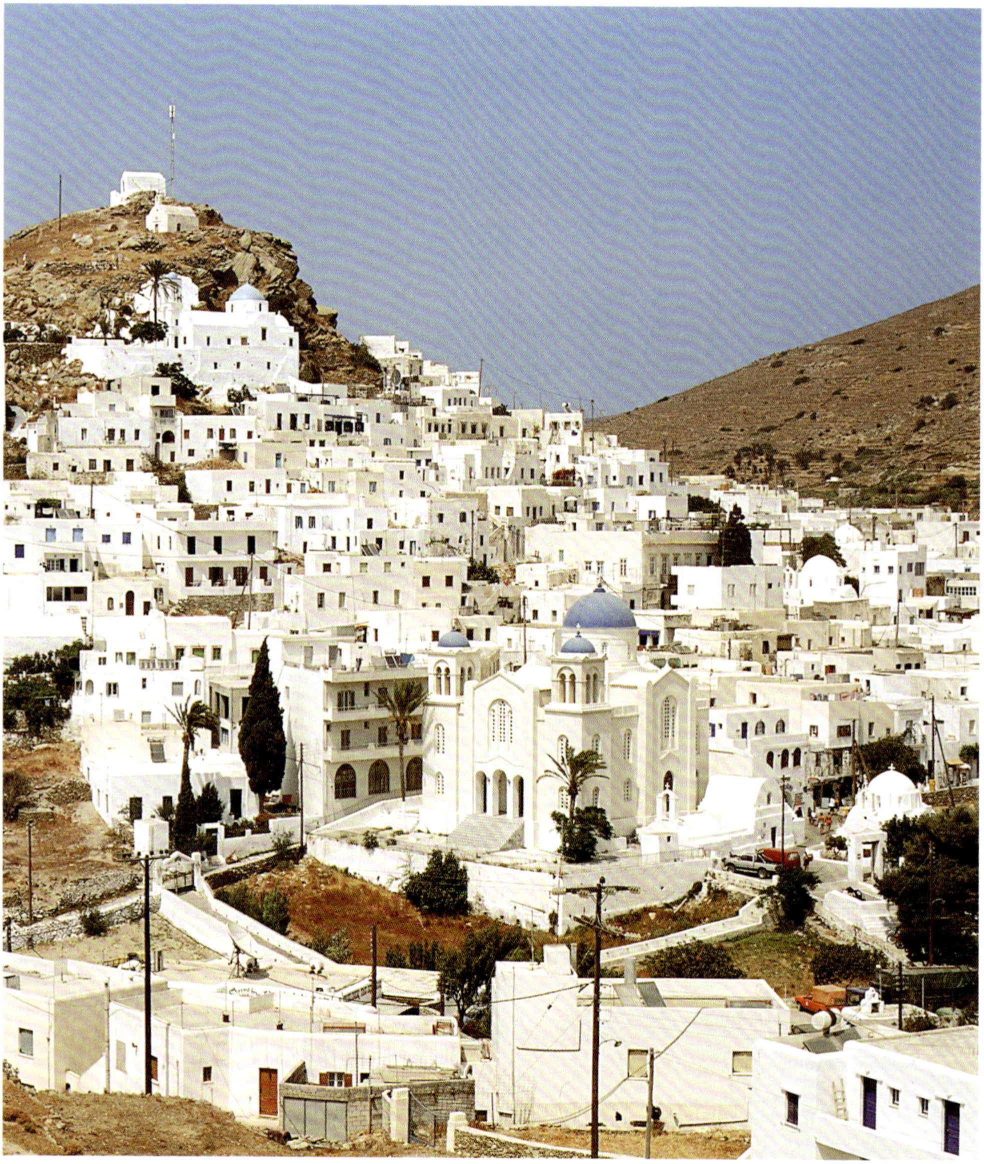

purposes as well. Led by a dictator, Muammar Qaddafi, infamous for his support of human rights abuses and international crimes, Libya has financially supported terrorism, backed ***rogue*** governments in other African nations, and pursued weapons of mass destruction. Recently, however, Libya vowed to abandon its past tyrannical ways.

Tunisia achieved independence from France in 1956 and continues to struggle for full democracy today. Tunisia began instituting reforms to improve women's lives long before any other North African country. Nevertheless, Tunisia's people continue to lack many freedoms. Political parties are very restricted, and human rights abuses continue to occur. Tunisia has achieved more economic and social stability than its neighbors, but infant mortality and unemployment rates remain high while literacy rates are quite low.

Algeria has faced serious difficulties since achieving independence from France in 1962. Algeria fought a grueling guerilla war for this independence. Political instability followed. In the early 1990s, serious civil strife broke out leading to 50,000 arrests and more than 100,000 deaths. Today, Algeria is picking up the pieces of its struggling government. At thirty-seven deaths per one thousand births, its infant mortality rate is the highest in the Mediterranean. Thirty-four percent of its work force is unemployed, and literacy remains low.

Since obtaining its independence from France and Spain, Morocco has also struggled in all of our measured areas. It currently shares last place with Egypt for having the lowest life expectancy rates in the Mediterranean region. Each has a life expectancy of approximately seventy years. Morocco also has the lowest literacy rates in the Mediterranean, and its infant mortality rate is above twenty deaths per one thousand births. To complicate issues, all of the North African countries have experienced huge migrations from rural areas to cities. People move from rural areas with hopes for a better quality of life, access to more services, and better prospects for jobs. This migration, however, has

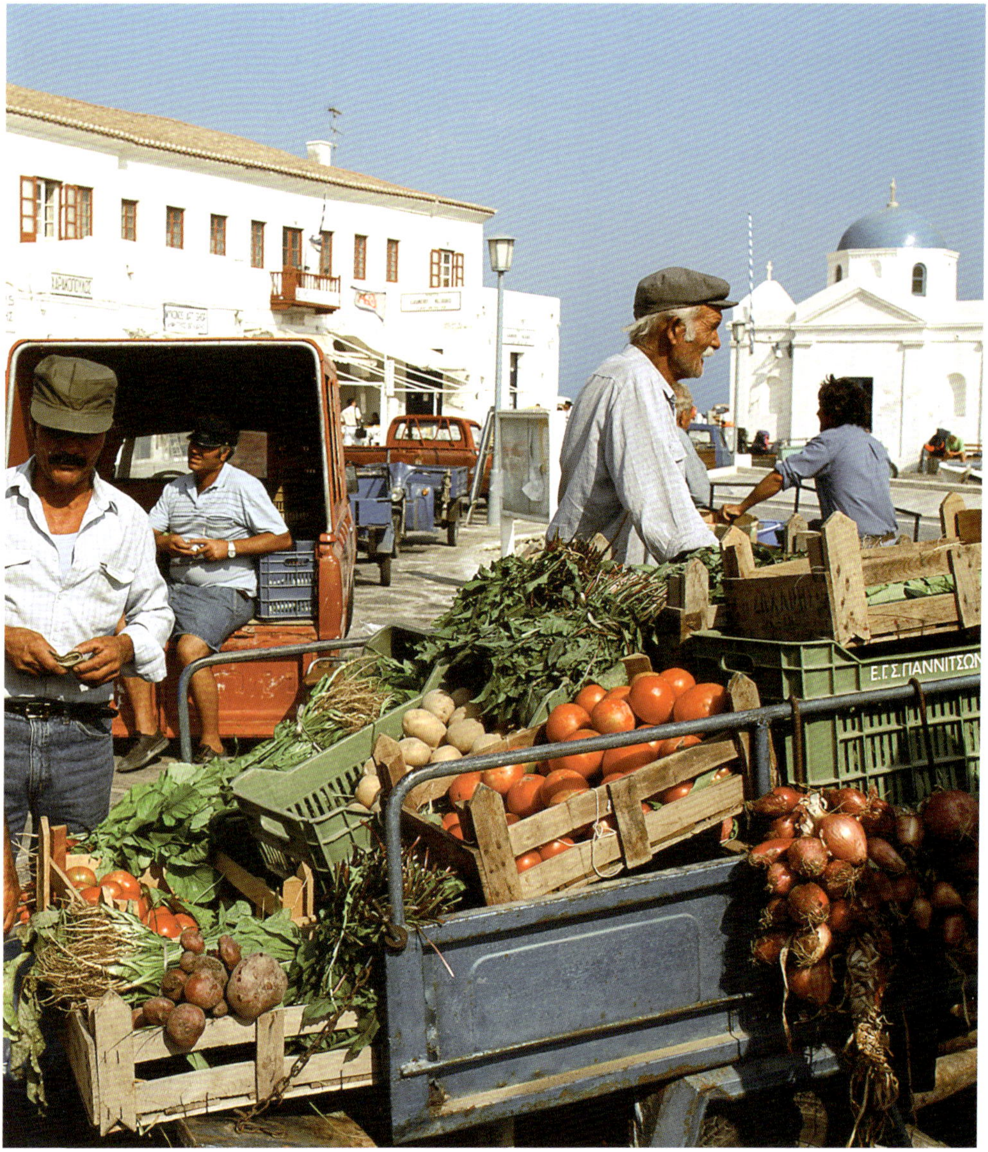

Farmers depend on their nations' infrastructures to get their crops to market.

happened so quickly that North African nations have not had the time or resources to develop adequate urban infrastructure to support the shifting population.

Now that we know a little more about the Mediterranean countries, we can begin to explore what women's lives are like in this region. To do this, however, we will need to look at more than just ***statistics***. Statistical indicators give us an idea about conditions in a certain area, but there's much they can't do. For instance, they can't tell us why conditions are the way they are or how individual people experience those conditions. Another way of learning about people's lives in a land far from your own is by studying history. All the conditions present in the world today are the result of circumstances in the past, and you don't have to look far to see how the events of yesteryear continue to affect life today. In fact, often the only way to understand present-day conditions is to learn about the historical events that brought today's conditions about.

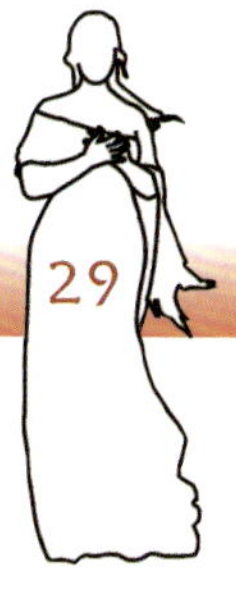

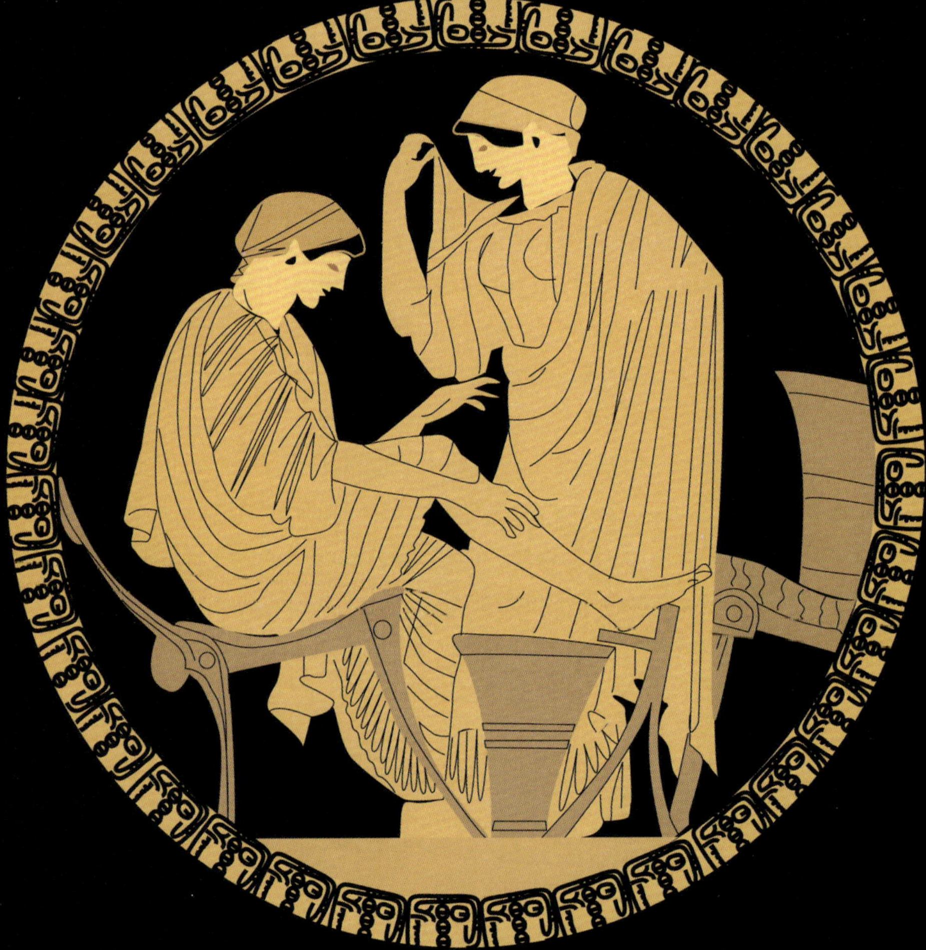

"[W]OMEN MUST PUT SOME EFFORT INTO THEMSELVES . . . MEN ARE NOT GOING TO CHANGE ANYTHING. IT'S NOT IN THEIR INTERESTS."
—OUARDIA, AN ALGERIAN WOMAN

2

WOMEN IN THE MEDITERRANEAN THROUGHOUT HISTORY

She marched through the streets, her robes swirling, the crowd swelling, and anger fueling her steps. The men who ruled Rome did a lot of frustrating things, but this time they had gone too far. Hortensia was fed up, and she was about to show it. Surprised guards moved to block her way. Paying them no heed, Hortensia and her entourage of seething noblewomen burst into the Roman Forum, a building which women never entered unless explicitly invited. The door to the ***triumvirate's*** chambers flew open as Hortensia boldly stepped forward and stated her demands. The triumvirate, however, wasn't going to take orders from mere women. "Cast them out!" they ordered the guards, but a mighty crowd had gathered and been stirred by Hortensia's speech. Fearing violence, the triumvirate was obliged to hear Hortensia out.

Hortensia's historic march to the Forum took place around 42 B.C.E. The Roman triumvirate had decided the best way to levy a tax without angering the Roman citizens would be to tax only the wealthiest women. At this time, Mediterranean women had few legal rights and no political representation, so the triumvirate expected their decision to pass virtually unnoticed. They made

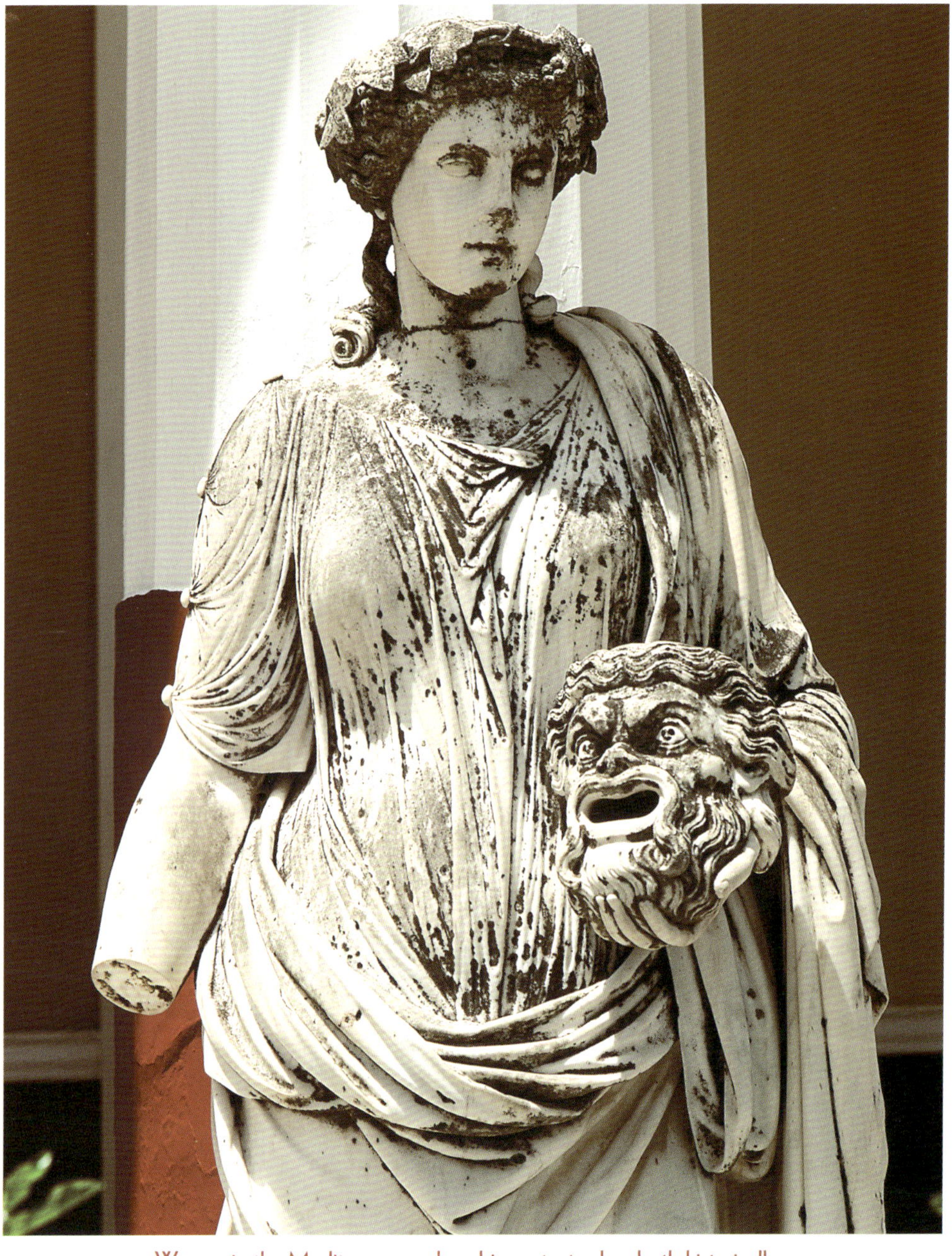

Women in the Mediterranean played important roles, both historically, in legend, and in artistic representations.

a bit of an error. Those women were enraged, especially since the tax was to support a civil war. Hortensia, who would become known as a great orator in Rome, marched up to the triumvirate and demanded that the tax be repealed. Why should women, she asked, who have no ability to participate in government and no equality with men, be made to finance the men's petty wars amongst each other? In the end, Hortensia would win only half her battle. The tax would not be fully repealed, but it was extended to men as well as women, a move that was one small step forward in Mediterranean women's battle for equality.

For thousands of years, the Mediterranean has been home to great civilizations and empires. The ancient Egyptian, Greek, and Roman empires (among others) all rose and fell in the lands surrounding the sea's shores. Many things you come in contact with every day originated in the Mediterranean. ***Architectural*** styles that today appear all over the world developed thousands of years ago in Greece and Rome. The stories of the Judeo-Christian Bible are based on events that occurred on the Mediterranean's eastern flank. The ***conquistadors*** who "discovered" and plundered the Americas were born on the Mediterranean's western shores. These are just a few examples of how the people of the Mediterranean have left ***indelible*** marks on the entire world and changed the course of world history.

While history is rich in tales of empires, explorers, warriors, and kings, it is lacking in stories about women. In most societies, women's activities were largely limited to the ***domestic*** sphere, and women had few opportunities in public life compared to their male counterparts. Like today, people in the past probably thought that battles were news, while the daily work of maintaining the house was not. Most of women's activities fell into the "not news" category and were not recorded. Furthermore, in times past, few people were educated. The vast majority of those educated people were religious men, and these men

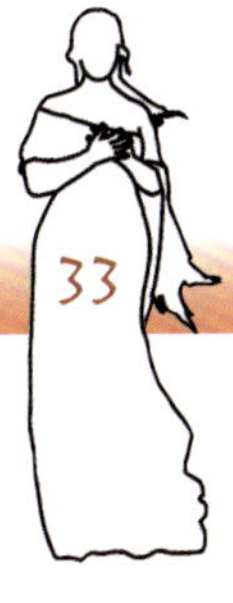

decided which texts were important enough to copy for future generations. Few writings made the cut. More women were probably educated and wrote than historical records indicate; few of their writings, however, were considered important enough to be copied and carried on through the ages.

Even when women were confined to the home, though, their influence was important. Throughout history, while men were off fighting battles, conquering their neighbors, searching for wealth in foreign lands, and ruling kingdoms, women were doing the work that kept people alive. This is not to say that men's accomplishments were not important, or that there weren't plenty of men who labored every day to support their families and communities, but the part women played in the continuation and advancement of societies cannot be overstated. If societies were machines, women would have been the hidden, hard-working parts that made things run.

Nevertheless, throughout Mediterranean history, women were generally considered inferior to men. They usually did not have the same legal rights as men, were expected to limit their activities to their homes, and had to be ***subservient*** to their husbands. The birth of boys was, in almost all cases, valued over the birth of girls. In many places, it was even customary for men to exclude their daughters from a count of their children. If asked how many children he had, a father would give only the number of sons.

Life in ancient times was extremely difficult, and much of life's daily labor fell to women. While husbands and children still slept, women rose before dawn to gather fuel, stoke household fires, fetch water from rivers or wells, grind grain, and bake the daily bread. Unlike today when we can turn on a tap for water, run to the store for bread, and put leftovers in the refrigerator to reheat the next day, in times past, the job of feeding a family began from scratch every day. Preparing food for the household, however, was only one of a woman's many labors. Making cloth, clothing, and blankets was another major

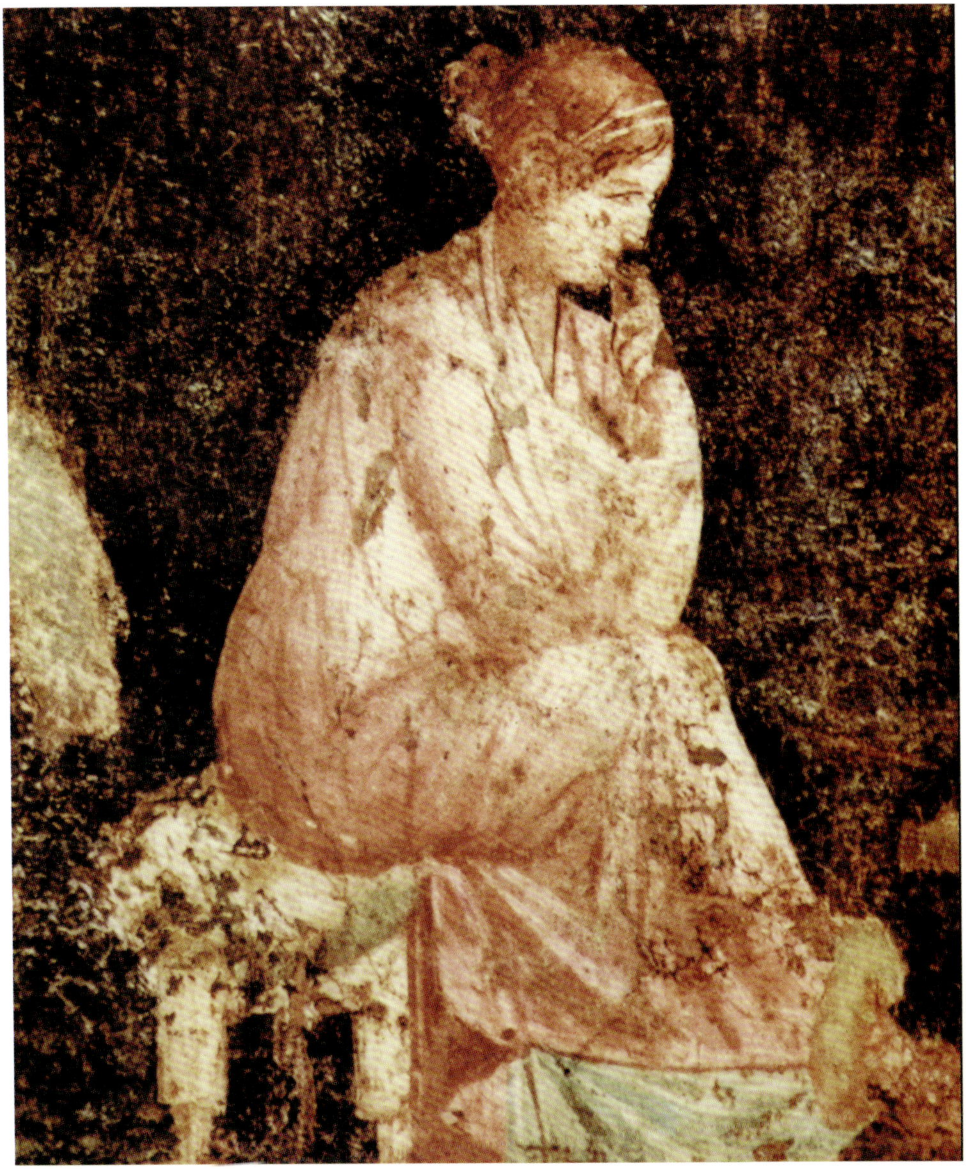

Women's lives in ancient Mediterranean regions were filled with labor. Only the very rich enjoyed the leisure portrayed here.

task. Spinning, weaving, and sewing were essential skills that women employed to keep their families clothed and warm, and these abilities were learned and practiced from a very young age. At just five years old, girls would already be learning certain skills and performing small tasks. In childhood, while their brothers were encouraged to romp and play games that enhanced their physical health and athletic prowess, girls learned to run a household.

A life built around domestic labor, however, did not necessarily mean that women were isolated within their homes, for many tasks lent themselves to group activities. For instance, in some parts of the Mediterranean, markets were women's realms where women acted both as the sellers and the purchasers of goods. Women also gathered on riverbanks or at other communal water sources to wash clothes. Cooking often took place outdoors, and tasks like *winnowing* and grinding grain could be performed in groups.

In modern North American society, both men and women are relatively free to choose independent paths for their lives based largely upon their personal desires. This social attitude, however, valuing an individual's desires, is a relatively recent phenomenon. For most of history (and still in many parts of the world today), the family was considered much more important than the individual, and people were expected to fulfill their social roles. For example, girls and boys generally had to marry the person their family wanted them to marry. Women were expected to devote themselves completely to their husbands and children. Self-sacrifice for the good of her family was assumed to be a woman's only natural attitude toward hardship and would therefore (it was believed) bring women natural happiness.

Mediterranean societies have traditionally been patriarchal and patrilocal, meaning that family authority was vested in the head male and that when a couple married, they went to live with the husband's side of the family. For a woman, this meant that after she married, she would leave her family and go to live in her husband's house. If her in-laws lived far away, she might never even visit her family again!

In the past, extended families usually lived together in the same house, so moving in with your husband also meant moving in with his parents, grandparents, his brothers and their wives, his unmarried sisters, and his nieces and

In the book **Women in Ancient Egypt**, Barbara Watterson lists four categories or social roles that women could fulfill in the ancient world. They are "goddess, devoted wife, doting mother, and scheming whore." Indeed, these four stereotypes of women can be found all over the world. Historically, in many areas, men could be anything from warriors to diplomats, kings to farmers, merchants to thieves, but women could only be these four things. What would a community usually think of a woman who wasn't devoted to her husband or didn't spend all of her time endlessly doting on her children? Well, chances are they didn't consider her a goddess.

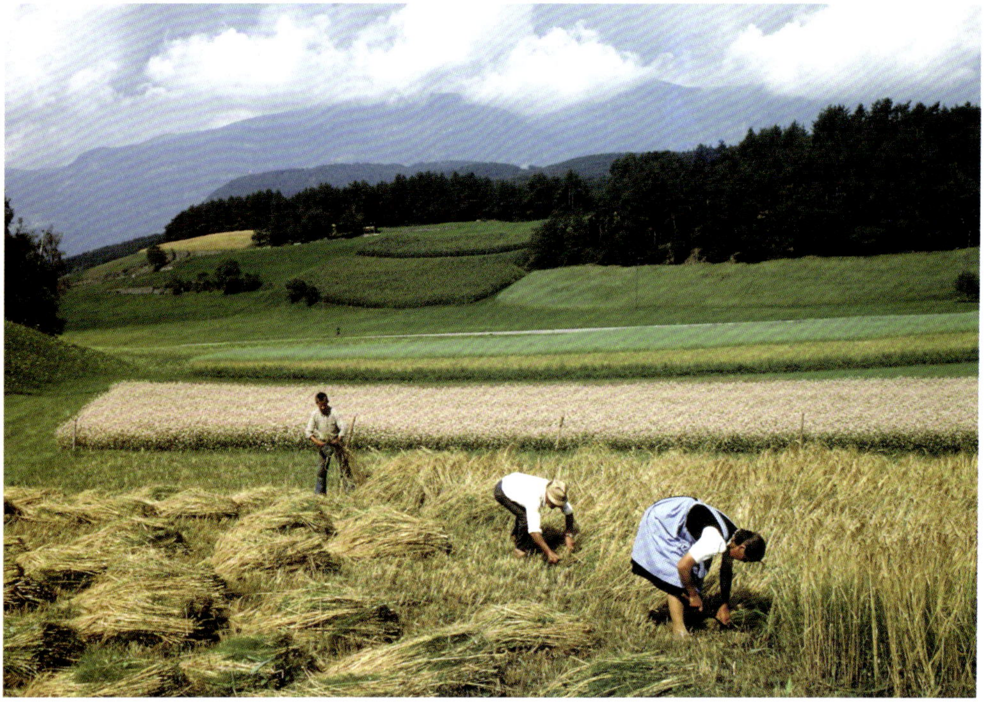

Many women in Mediterranean countries work alongside men doing farm labor.

nephews. The most important person in a new bride's life was not her husband (though of course she was expected to be obedient and attentive to him) but her mother-in-law. Though the patriarch was the supreme authority figure of a family, his wife directed all the work within a household, and all the women of the house would be subject to her will and expected to obey her direction. A new bride was generally the lowest person in the family hierarchy, and her status would only improve with the arrival of the next bride or with the birth of sons.

Women in Ancient Egypt

Attitudes toward women in the ancient Mediterranean, however, were not universal. Women's opportunities, status, and roles changed over time and from place to place. Even within a single society, all women did not usually occupy the same role. One of the most important things that determined what a woman's life would be like was her ***socioeconomic status***. A woman of the lower classes would have a very difficult life defined by hard work. A woman of the upper classes would have a life made easier by the labor of slaves and servants. In the book *Women in Ancient Egypt*, author Barbara Watterson discusses ancient Egypt as a place of relative freedom for women. This ancient Mediterranean society granted the same legal rights to women as to men. The catch was that different socioeconomic groups were treated differently under the law. Therefore, a female slave would have the same legal rights (which were just about none) as a male slave. A female peasant had the same legal rights as a male peasant. A female ***aristocrat*** had the same legal rights as a male aristocrat. These groups, however, had different legal rights from each other.

Women in ancient Egypt, if members of the appropriate class, could own, inherit, purchase, sell, and pass property on to their children. Women enjoyed a good deal of physical freedom, being able to move about unchaperoned. Ancient Egyptian society also differed from other Mediterranean societies in that ***lineage*** was traced through the mother's line rather than the father's. Egyptian society was still patriarchal, but sons were known by the name of their mother rather than their father. This is similar to Jewish society, in which Jewish heritage is passed to children from the mother. In ancient Egypt, women also had the option of a few career paths beyond the usual roles of wives and mothers. According to Watterson, women could also be priestesses, midwives, professional mourners, dancers, or musicians. Furthermore, love between

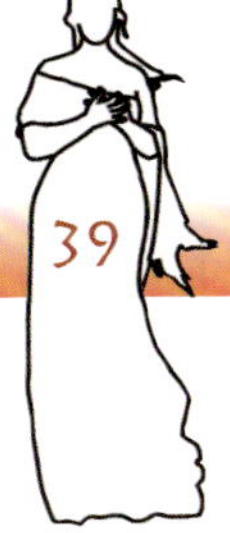

men and women was valued and desired by ancient Egyptians. Love, mutual respect, and the individual's desires may have played a role in the selection of marriage partners.

WOMEN IN ANCIENT GREECE

Women's position in ancient Greece was far different from their roles in ancient Egypt. In Greece, women had few legal rights and were expected to remain in the home. When they did go out, they had to wear head coverings and be escorted. Even within the home, Greek women were often chaperoned and confined to women's quarters. Still, within Greece, women's situations varied from place to place. Ancient Greece was not a united country the way we normally think of countries today. Rather, Greece consisted of many different city-states that were politically independent and often fought each other in internal wars. Two very prominent Greek city-states in ancient times were Athens and Sparta. These two cities were rivals of a sort with different ways of life and philosophies. One great difference between the cities was in their attitudes toward women.

Considered the center of Greek culture and philosophy, Athens was a very conservative place. Athenians valued the arts, education, and intellectual inquiry. Sparta, on the other hand, was defined by its military. Though Spartans valued art and education, the most important art was the art of war, and physical strength and athleticism were highly valued. One might expect that women would be more respected in a place like Athens than in a society built around physical strength and warfare, but in fact the opposite was true. In Athens, not only were women not well respected, they were considered mentally deficient, childlike, and in need of constant supervision. Each Greek woman in Athens had a male guardian called a *kyrios* who oversaw all aspects of her life. Before marriage, this kyrios would usually be her father. By today's standards, Athenian women married very young, usually in their early teens. At this point, a woman's

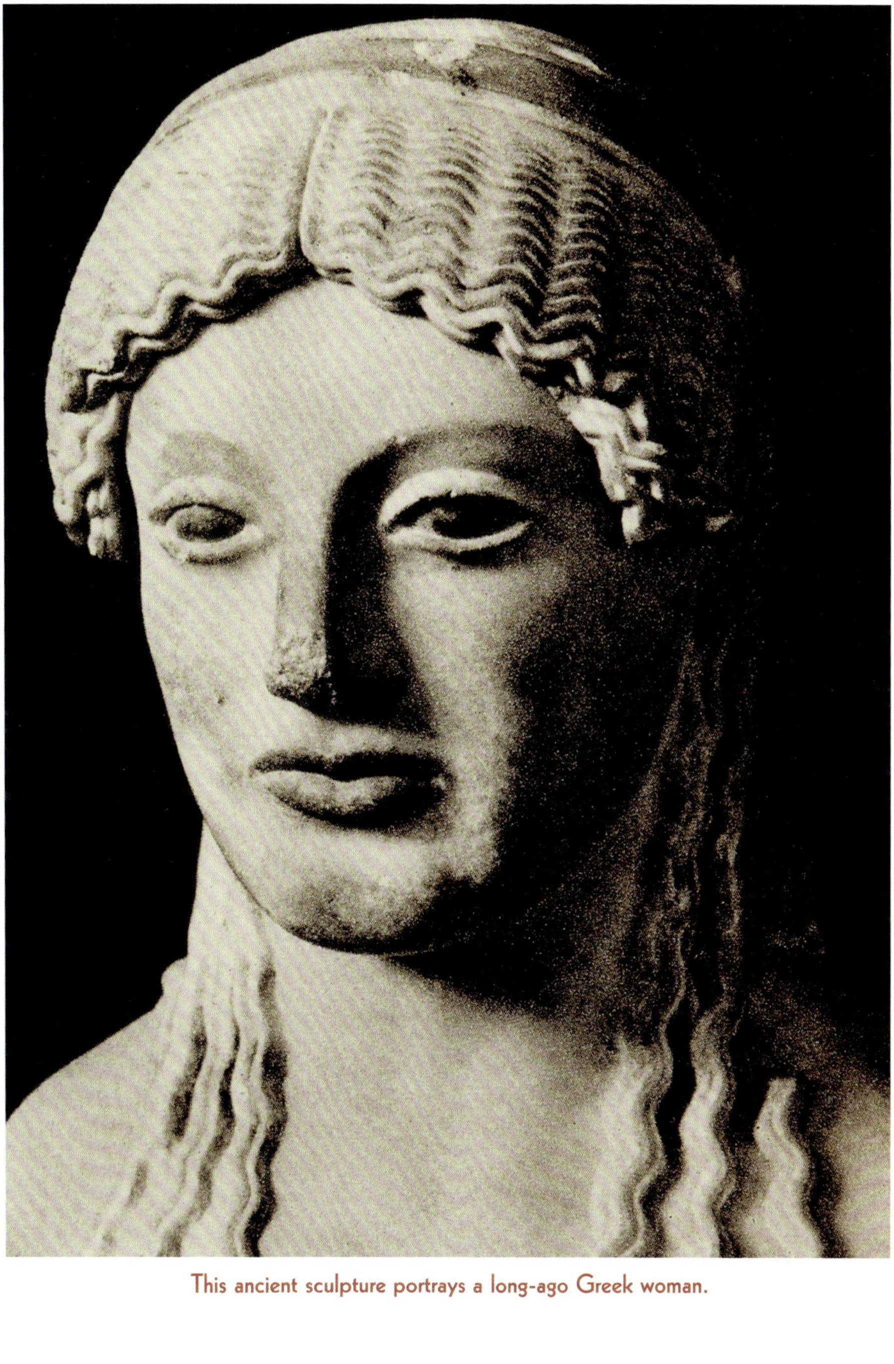

This ancient sculpture portrays a long-ago Greek woman.

husband (who was usually much older than her and often twice her age) became her kyrios. An unmarried woman's kyrios could also be her brother or another close male relative, and a widow's kyrios would often be her son.

Not only was an Athenian woman always supervised, she was also expected to be largely silent and completely deferential to men. She could own personal items like clothing and jewelry, but she had no right to either purchase or sell such property. By law, she was only allowed to handle as much money as it would take to buy about a week's worth of flour. Any larger financial transaction had to be handled by a man.

Spartan women had a very different experience than women elsewhere in Greece. Sparta's militaristic state society was deeply divided according to ***gender***, but these gender divisions actually gave women much freedom. From the age of just seven years old, all men were part of the military and lived separately from their families. With men so absent from the home, women were left to run much of the Spartan society. They could freely own, buy, and sell not only goods like clothing and jewelry but even land. Girls were required to go to school and were encouraged to enter athletic competition. Marriage also occurred much later for Spartan girls, who usually married at eighteen.

Spartan women were known throughout Greece for their strength and athletic physiques. They were also ***infamous*** for being bold and sharp-tongued. Bravery and strength were extremely important to Spartans, and women took as much pride in the Spartan military philosophy as did men. Women openly mocked men who were cowardly in battle. While in other parts of the Mediterranean adultery was a crime punishable by death, many Spartan women had lovers other than their husbands. It appears, however, that these arrangements may have been the result of a declining population and an attempt by Spartans to produce more children rather than a display of the society's openness and acceptance of women's physical freedom.

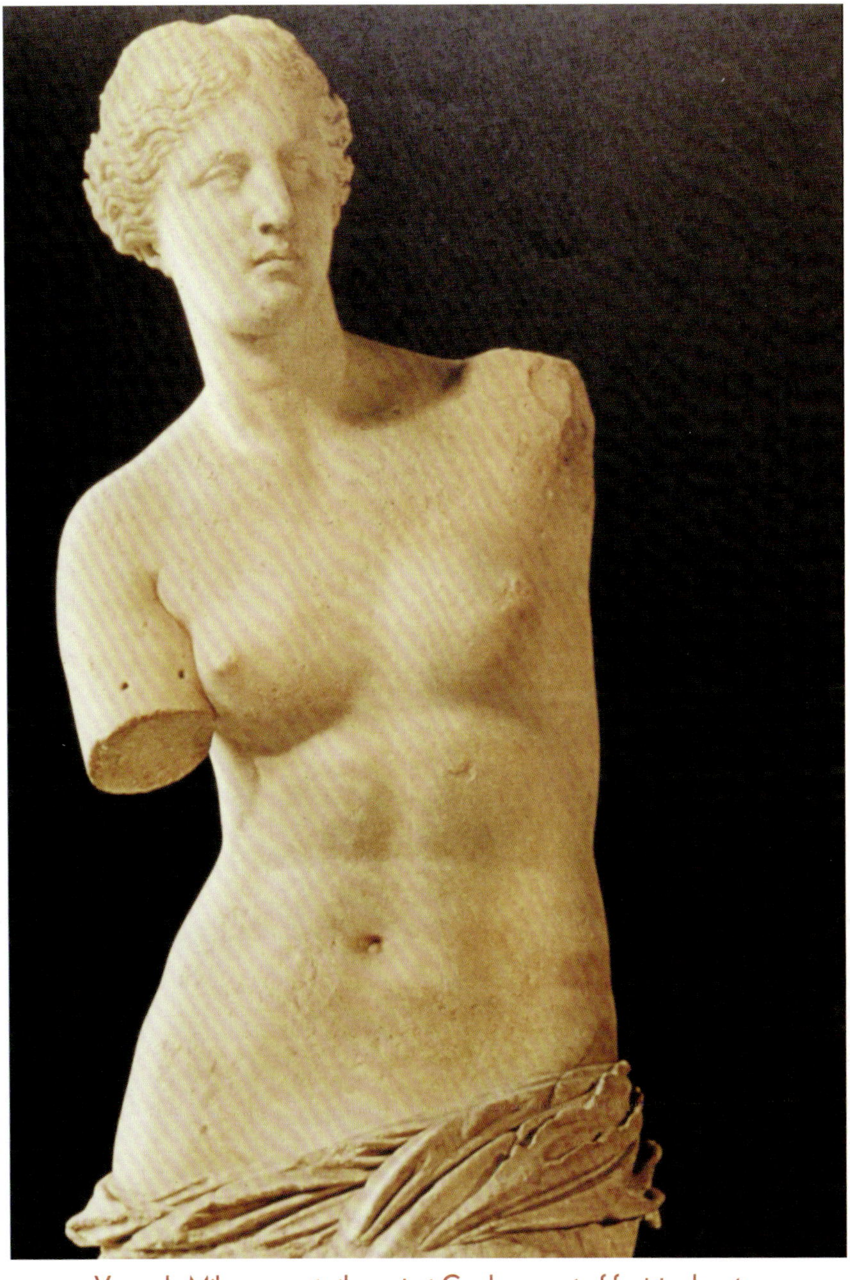

Venus de Milo represents the ancient Greek concept of feminine beauty.

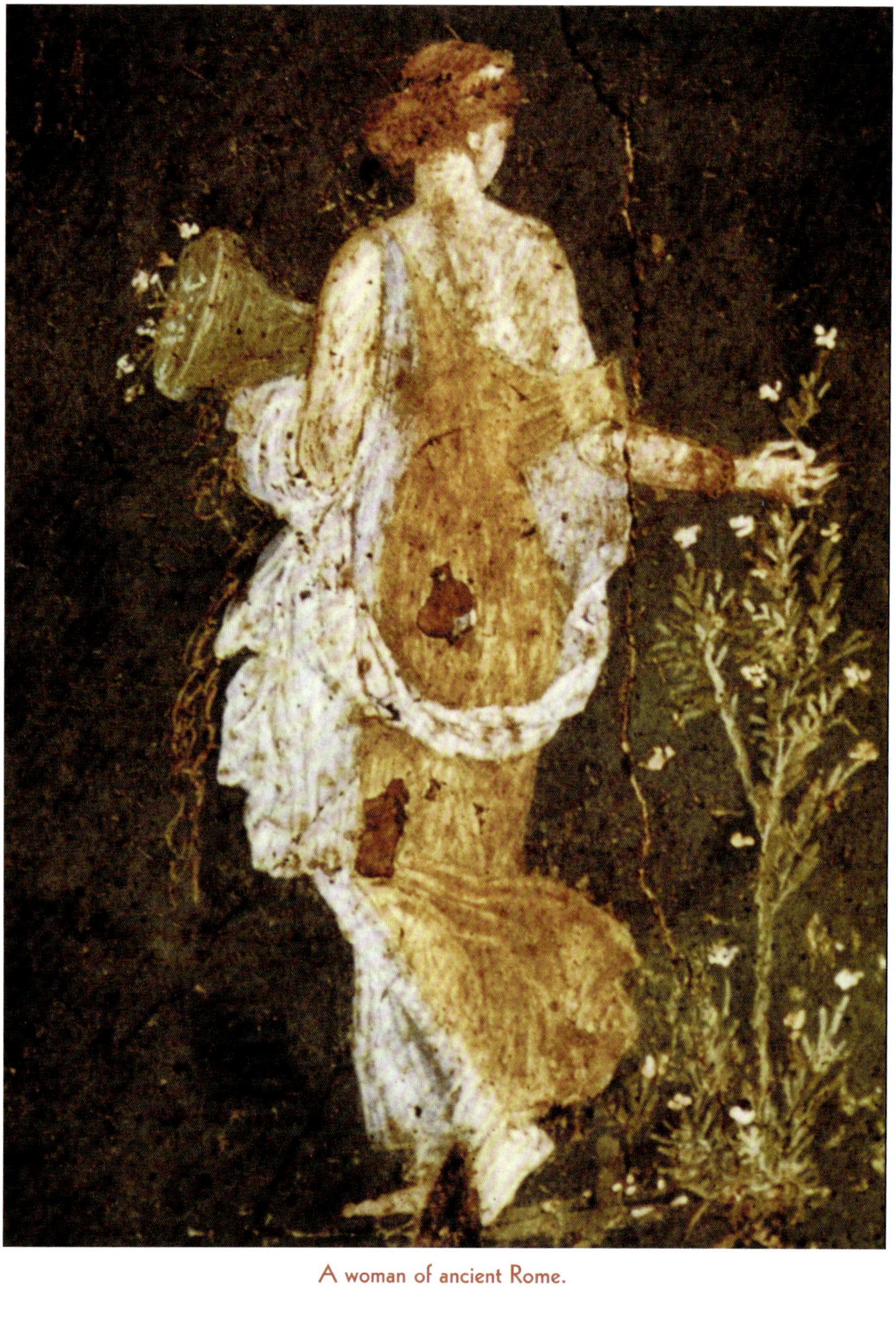

A woman of ancient Rome.

Despite all the freedoms Spartan women enjoyed, they were still second-class citizens. Though women's opinions were more respected in Sparta and value was placed on giving girls at least some education, women still could not participate directly in government or hold any type of public office. Women were valued by the Spartan state, but in the end, this value was not for the women as individuals, but for women as the creators of more Spartans—specifically more Spartan warriors. For example, the value Spartans placed on later marriage had nothing to do with ideas about women's happiness or rights. Rather, Spartans realized that women bore healthier children and had better survival rates in childbirth if they physically matured before marrying and having children. Like everywhere else in the ancient world, a woman's worth in Sparta was, in the end, based on her ability to produce children.

WOMEN IN ANCIENT ROME

As we learned from Hortensia's story, women in ancient Rome had few rights. In fact, they were not much better off than women were in Athens. Women in Rome had to be supervised by a man—generally their fathers and then their husbands—and could not participate in public life or hold any government office. While lower-class women usually had to work to support their families, upper-class women were barred from working. Marriages were arranged, and girls married while still very young, generally by their mid-teens.

Adultery in Rome, as in other places, was an extremely serious crime, though it was generally more serious for the married woman than for the man. A father had the right to kill his daughter and the person she was committing adultery with if they were found committing the crime in his home. A husband could likewise kill his wife and her lover. A woman could never kill her husband, but she could seek a divorce if she could prove he was committing adultery. In this respect, Roman divorce law was more liberal than in other areas of the Mediterranean, where only men had the right to initiate divorce.

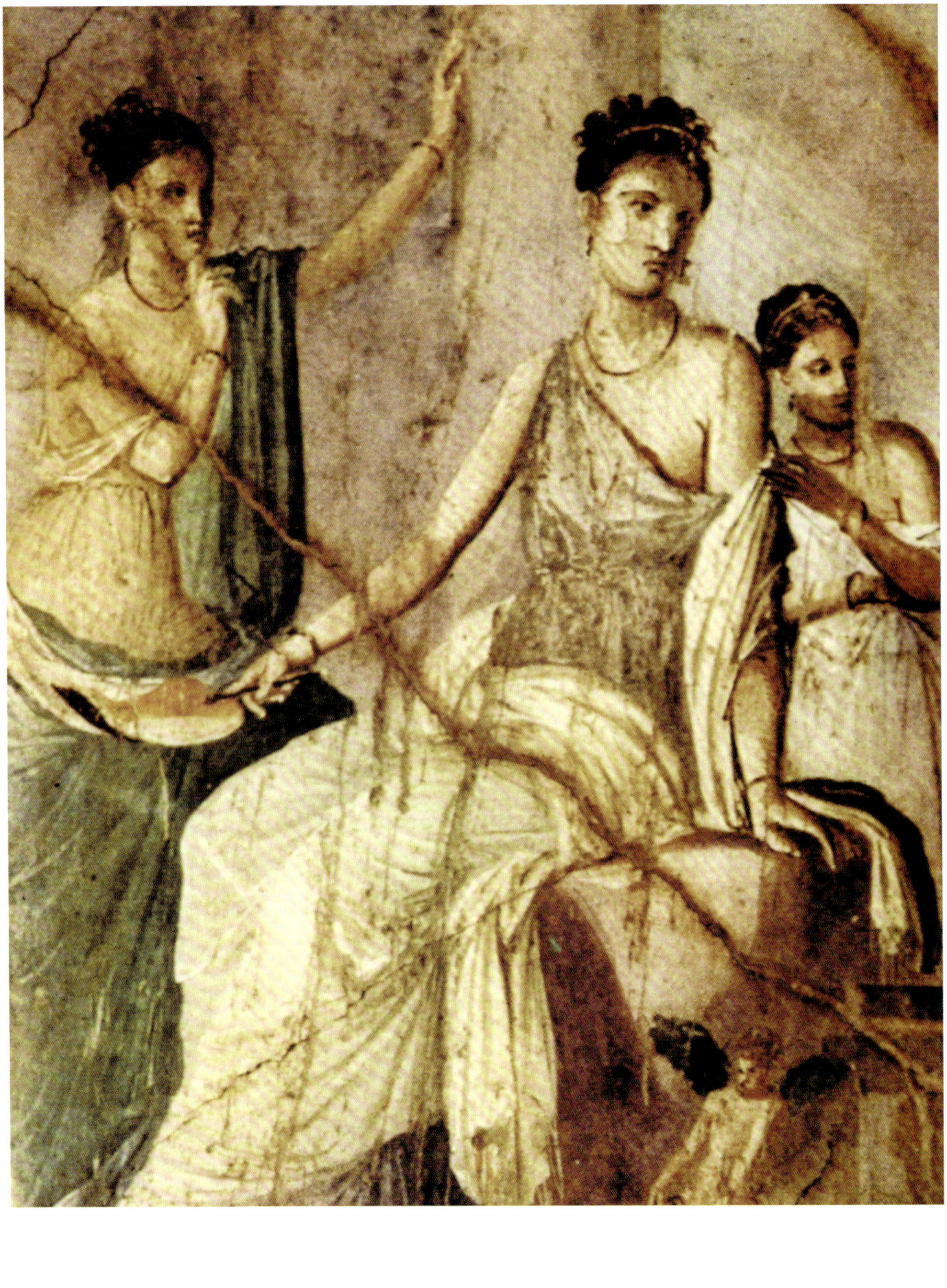

Though laws governing women's behavior in Rome were very strict, society may have been more relaxed than the laws would suggest. Over centuries, women in Rome tested their boundaries and pushed for change. Eventually, women gained greater power over property and greater freedom in their marriages. Women like Hortensia agitated for more rights and exerted some influence, even in government. Examples like Hortensia's, however, were few and far between. Though changes may have occurred in practice, they were not reflected in the laws, which remained very strict. In many ways, the situation for Mediterranean women would remain the same well into the twentieth century.

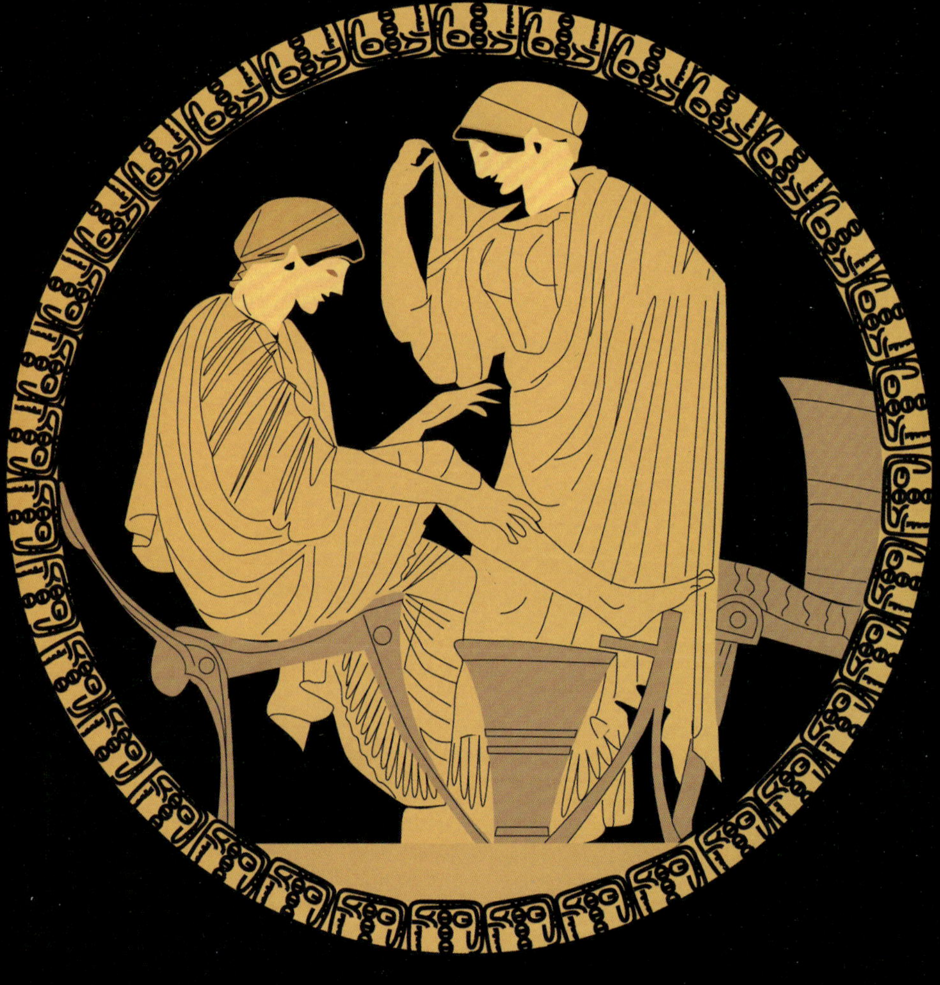

"LOCAL, NATIONAL, REGIONAL AND GLOBAL PEACE IS ATTAINABLE AND IS INEXTRICABLY LINKED WITH THE ADVANCEMENT OF WOMEN."
—BEIJING DECLARATION, UNITED NATIONS, FOURTH WORLD CONFERENCE ON WOMEN

3

WOMEN IN THE MEDITERRANEAN TODAY

In some parts of the Mediterranean, social changes, education, new technologies, and economic advancements have given women more freedom, time, opportunities, and equality than they've ever had before. In other areas of the Mediterranean, however, women's lives are still governed by the same hard labor, familial duties, and restrictive laws and customs that defined the lives of their sisters so long ago.

CEDAW AND WHAT IT MEANS FOR WOMEN

Around the world, focus on women's circumstances has greatly increased in recent years. In the last three decades, many members of the international community began to see women's advancement and equality as a top priority. To this end, global efforts have been made at improving women's situations in education, health, society, the economy, and government.

The United Nations has worked at the heart of these global efforts. In 1979, a huge step toward equal rights for women was made in something called the Convention on the Elimination of All Forms of Discrimination Against Women (or CEDAW). Many people call the CEDAW "an international bill of rights for women." This is a very good description. The CEDAW is an international treaty that demands an end to all forms of discrimination against women. Once a country has accepted the treaty, it is required to act according to the treaty's principles, put laws into place to protect women and ensure their equality, and submit reports on their progress at least every four years. The United Nations' Web site lists three of the main responsibilities countries take on by accepting CEDAW. They are:

1. To incorporate the principle of equality of men and women in their legal system, abolish all discriminatory laws, and adopt appropriate ones prohibiting discrimination against women.

2. To establish tribunals and other public institutions to ensure the effective protection of women against discrimination.

3. To ensure elimination of all acts of discrimination against women by persons, organizations, or enterprises.

To date, every Mediterranean country except Monaco has accepted CEDAW. However, this does not mean that gender equality has been achieved in the region. Some Mediterranean countries accepted CEDAW much later than others, countries have varying levels of commitment to the agreement, and some lack the resources to implement the changes CEDAW requires. Wars and *civil* strife have sapped some area's resources, and efforts toward advancing women's rights have fallen (at least temporarily) by the wayside in the wake of life and death struggles. Bosnia and Herzegovina, Serbia and Montenegro, Lebanon, and Syria are all party to the convention, but none of these countries have submitted the required reports on their progress in implementing the convention's principles.

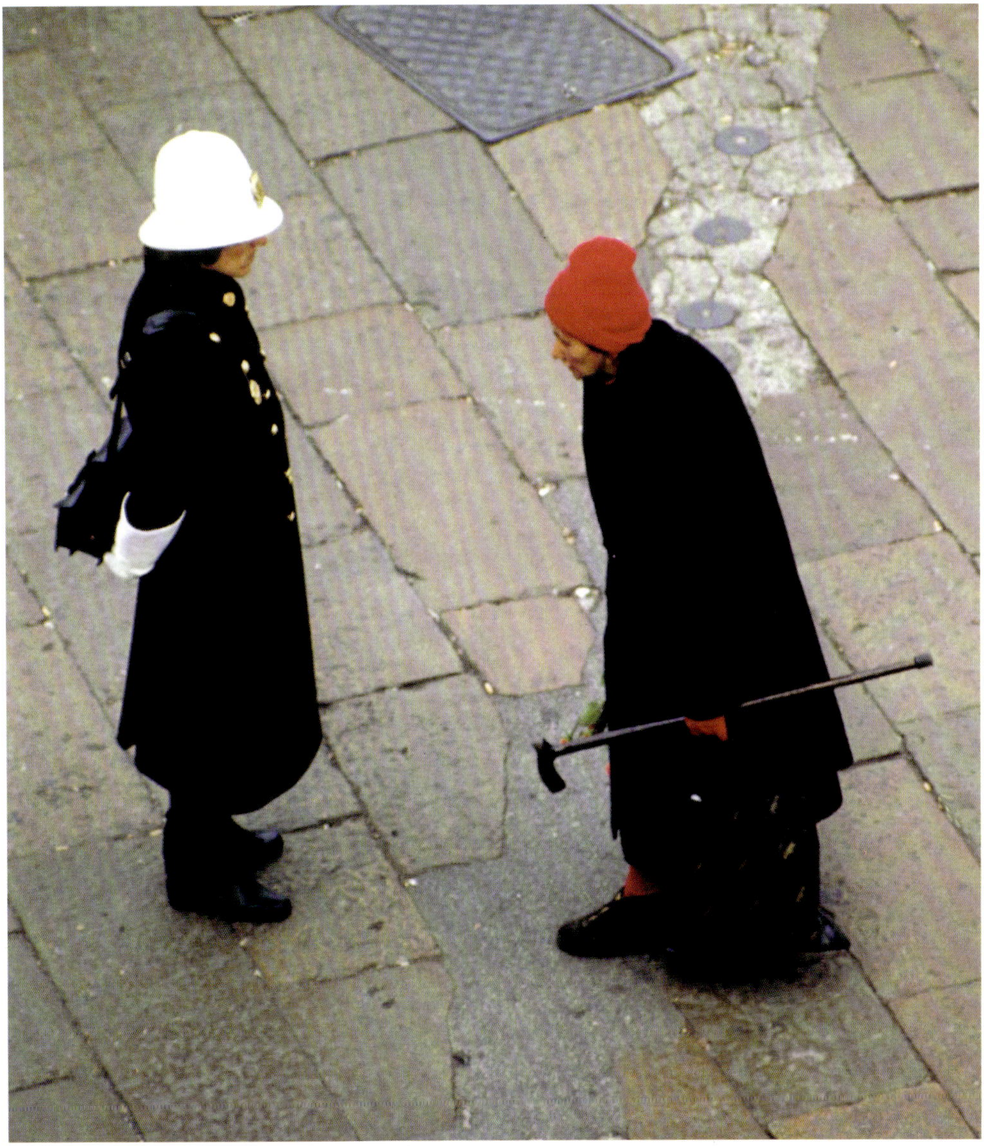

A woman in a Mediterranean public square speaks with a guard.

Lawmakers can sign conventions, and governments can proclaim new attitudes, but populations are often slow to change their ways—especially when it comes to something as deeply ingrained as discrimination against women. In some countries, the official laws have changed, but actual practices have not. Even in countries that have been committed to gender equality for decades, challenges still persist. In places where gender equality is a relatively new social value, some women aren't even aware that there are laws guaranteeing their equality and protecting them from discrimination and violence. Even when women do know their rights, they often have no one to appeal to if those rights have been violated.

WOMEN AND EDUCATION

Equal education is a fundamental step toward gender equality. In chapter 1, we talked about literacy rates as quality-of-life indicators. One of the reasons education is so important is because it helps people to advance within a society by qualifying them for good-paying jobs with safe working conditions. When literacy rates are low, very few people are able to qualify for the types of work that would improve their quality of life. Low literacy rates can also mean that certain groups of people, like the poor, minorities, or females, don't have access to education.

Of all the Mediterranean countries, those in North Africa have historically had the lowest literacy rates in the region, especially for women. The North African numbers post huge disparities between female and male literacy. At one time in Algeria, for example, 50 percent of men were illiterate, while a whopping 80 percent of women were illiterate! Egypt and Morocco had almost exactly the same numbers. Although literacy rates in Mediterranean Asia have historically been much higher than in North Africa, they still showed troubling disparities between females and males. Statistics like these drew a lot of attention from the international community, and in recent years many efforts have focused on improving girls' access to education.

In response to national and international efforts, Mediterranean Asian and North African countries have made huge strides in women's education. Today, both women and men under the age of twenty-four have much higher literacy rates than their parents. The gap between women's and men's literacy, though still existent, is not as wide as it once was. Nevertheless, in some areas, girls still have very low participation in school, often attending only from age six to about ten or eleven.

There are many contributing factors to girls' low school participation. One is prevailing attitudes that education is just for boys, but other reasons are more practical. Some rural areas simply don't have schools, and parents are far less willing to send their daughters than their sons to a boarding school in another town. Another reason is that many families can't see a benefit in educating their daughters. In areas where there are still no economic opportunities for women

"[I]n our area, women don't go out."

—Fatima, an Algerian woman, discussing life in her rural village.

(**Women of the Mediterranean**, edited by Monique Gadant)

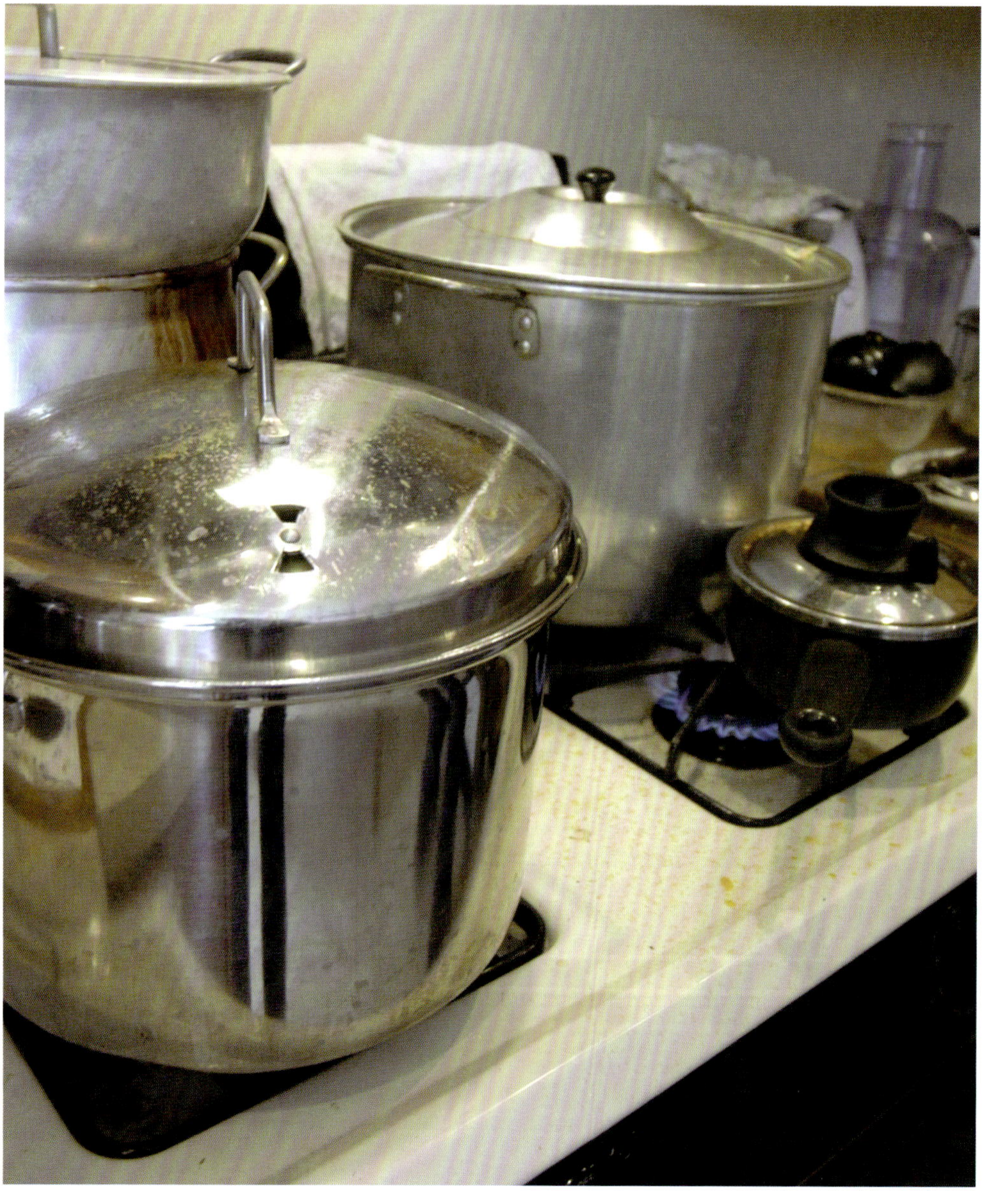

Preparing meals takes up a large part of many Mediterranean women's days.

and a woman's only choice is to get married and have children, people ask, "What good will it be to have an educated daughter who then has nothing to apply her education to?" If women had the education, however, they could begin opening doors for themselves. They could put their knowledge and skills toward creating new opportunities where none currently exist. Perhaps this, the threat of change and women seizing control of their own futures, is another reason why people are slow to send their daughters to school.

The situation for women and education is generally better in Mediterranean Europe. Today, almost 100 percent of the European population under age twenty-four is literate, and there is virtually no gap between women's and men's literacy. High-quality education is in most cases free and mandatory until the age of sixteen. In some countries, like Italy, girls even have higher enrollment, stay in school longer, and earn more degrees than boys. France also has an exceptional educational system. There, free education is available beginning at the age of two!

WOMEN IN THE WORKFORCE AND PUBLIC LIFE

Today, Mediterranean women work as doctors, lawyers, business owners, cooks, factory workers, teachers, taxi drivers, artists, musicians, and just about every other job you can imagine. Nevertheless, as is the case with education, women's participation and opportunities in the workforce are by no means equal to those of men. Many people realize that women's contributions to business and the private sector are a vital part of successful economies and the elimination of poverty. In recognition of this, developing nations are concentrating on increasing women's meaningful participation in the economy.

What continues to be troubling both in the Mediterranean region and around the world is that despite women's gains in education, many women are still barred from success in the workforce and participation in public life. In Mediterranean Asia and North Africa, women's participation in the economy has improved, but not nearly as much as one would expect based on the strides in education. Usually when a country's women have access to education, other measurements of their equality (like access to meaningful employment and political participation) also improve, but this has not been so in Mediterranean Asia and North Africa.

Discriminatory attitudes continue to bar many women from successful employment. In areas with high unemployment rates, many people think that it would be better for women to stay home and leave the few jobs that are available for men. Although most countries in the Mediterranean have laws to protect women's rights within and outside of the home, discrimination in hiring is common. Even when women work outside of the home, few are in managerial positions or other jobs with lots of authority. Today, men still hold most of the managerial jobs and are largely in charge of hiring. Not only do some people in charge of hiring think that it's better for women to stay home and leave the jobs for the men, they also think that hiring a woman is a waste of time. They believe that female employees will just get married, have children, and quit their jobs anyway. It can be very difficult for women to overcome such stereotypes.

Few Mediterranean women are self-employed or business owners. A major reason for this is that banks are less willing to give loans to women than to men. This discrimination in lending is pervasive around the world, and many countries now have programs and organizations that focus on obtaining ***start-up capital*** for women's businesses. Egypt recently initiated such a program and hopes that women's businesses will increase.

As is the case in the rest of the world, throughout the Mediterranean, women continue to make less money than men even when they are performing the same jobs, have the same education, and are putting in the same amount of time as their male counterparts. Women face greater barriers to advancement and promotion. To make matters more difficult, women's responsibilities in the home have not decreased, resulting in women, on average, having less leisure

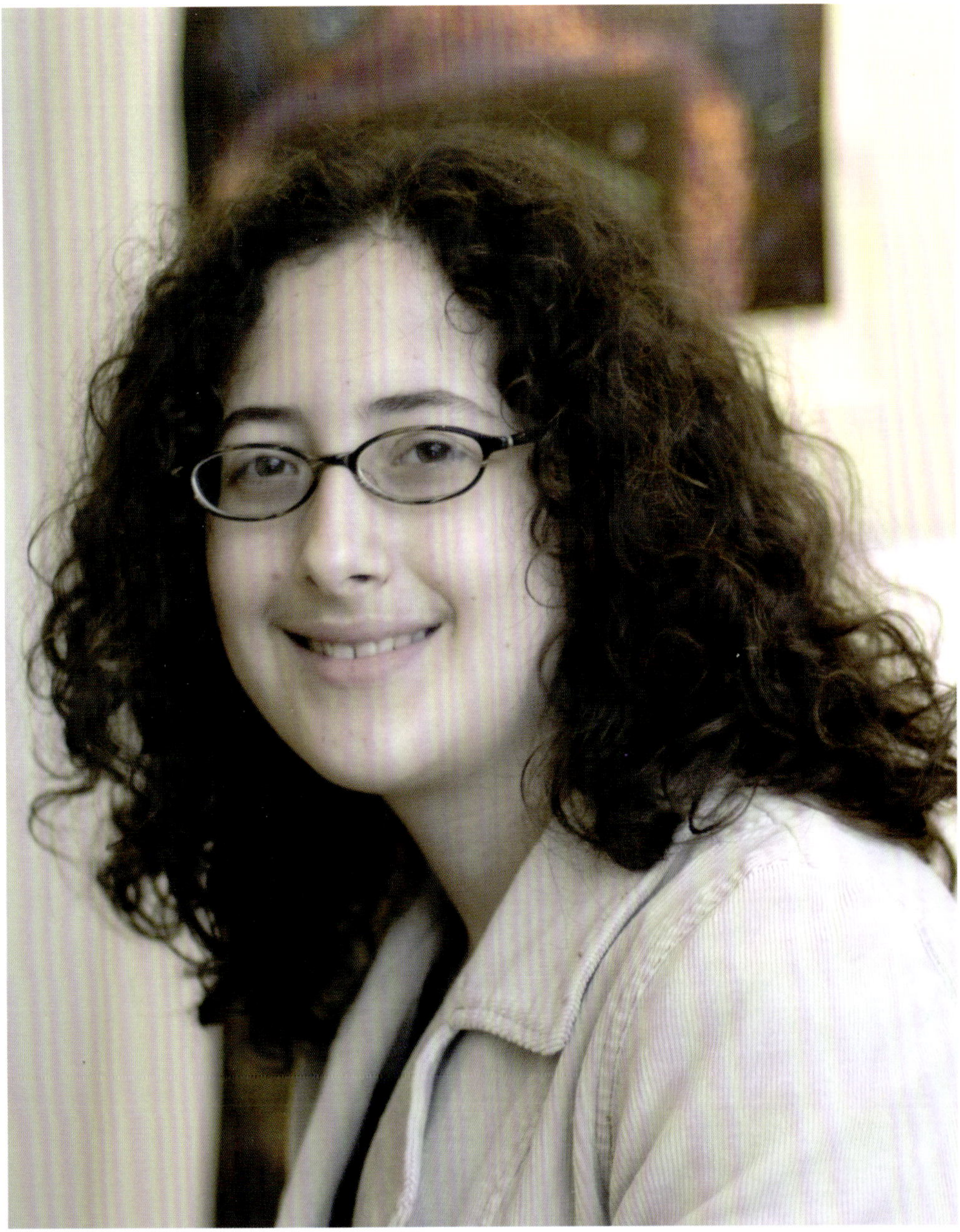

A young Italian woman has far more opportunities than women of Mediterranean Africa and Asia.

time than men and more difficulty balancing their working schedules with their home life.

Mediterranean women also have lower political participation and representation than men. Women's participation in public and political life in Mediterranean Asia and North Africa are exceptionally low. While having the fastest rates of female-education improvement, these regions still have the lowest female political participation rates of any region in the world. Female leaders who would like to see more women becoming active in politics believe that it is women themselves who will have to force political changes. Women have the right to vote in every Mediterranean country, but in many places women's voter-turnout continues to be much lower than men's. Many leaders believe that, for the gender distribution in politics to change, women especially must

Currently, countries that achieve 30 percent representation for women in political bodies are considered to be doing very well, but many women today are questioning why they should be satisfied with 30 percent participation when they make up more than 50 percent of the world's population.

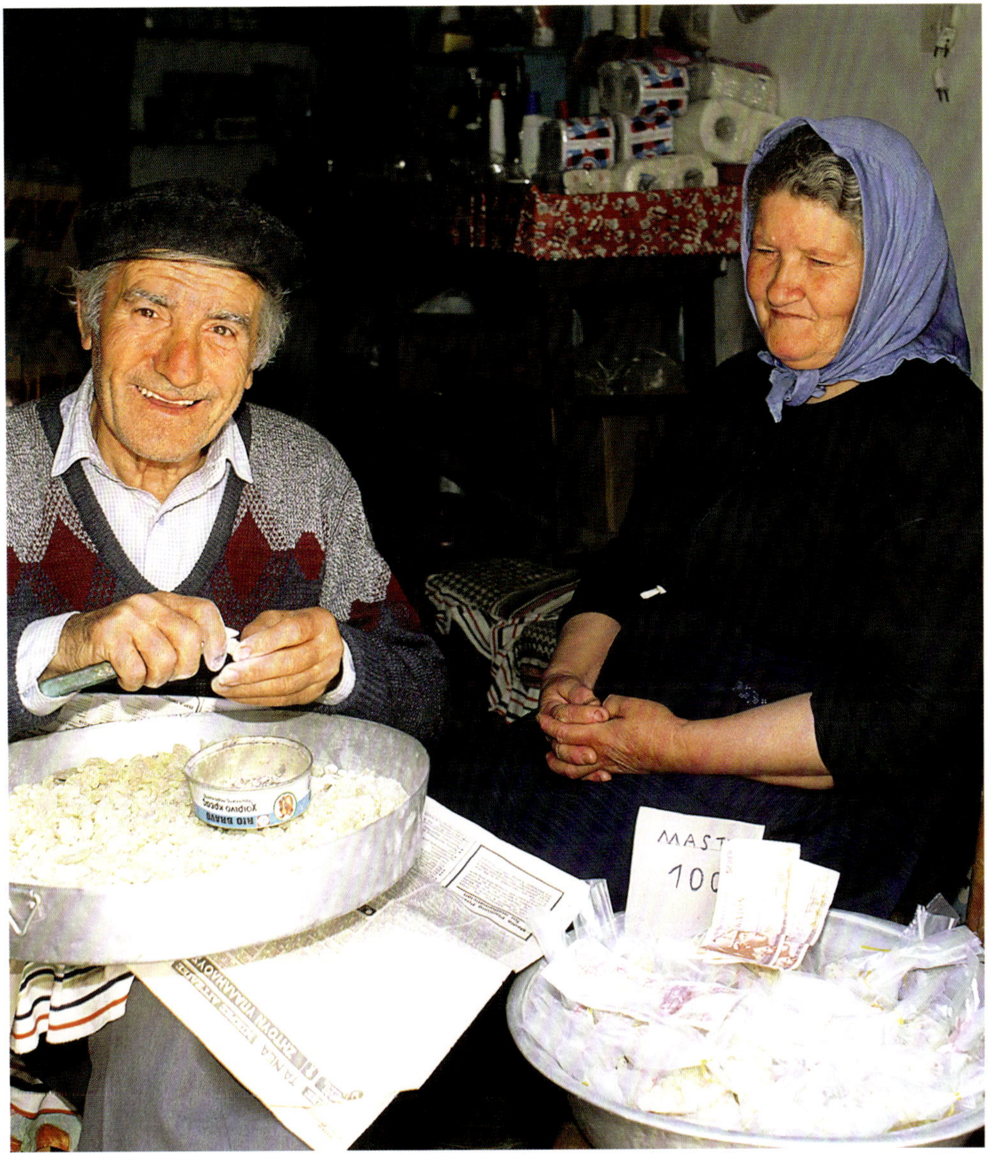

Most Mediterranean businesses are owned and run by men; women are more apt to play supporting roles.

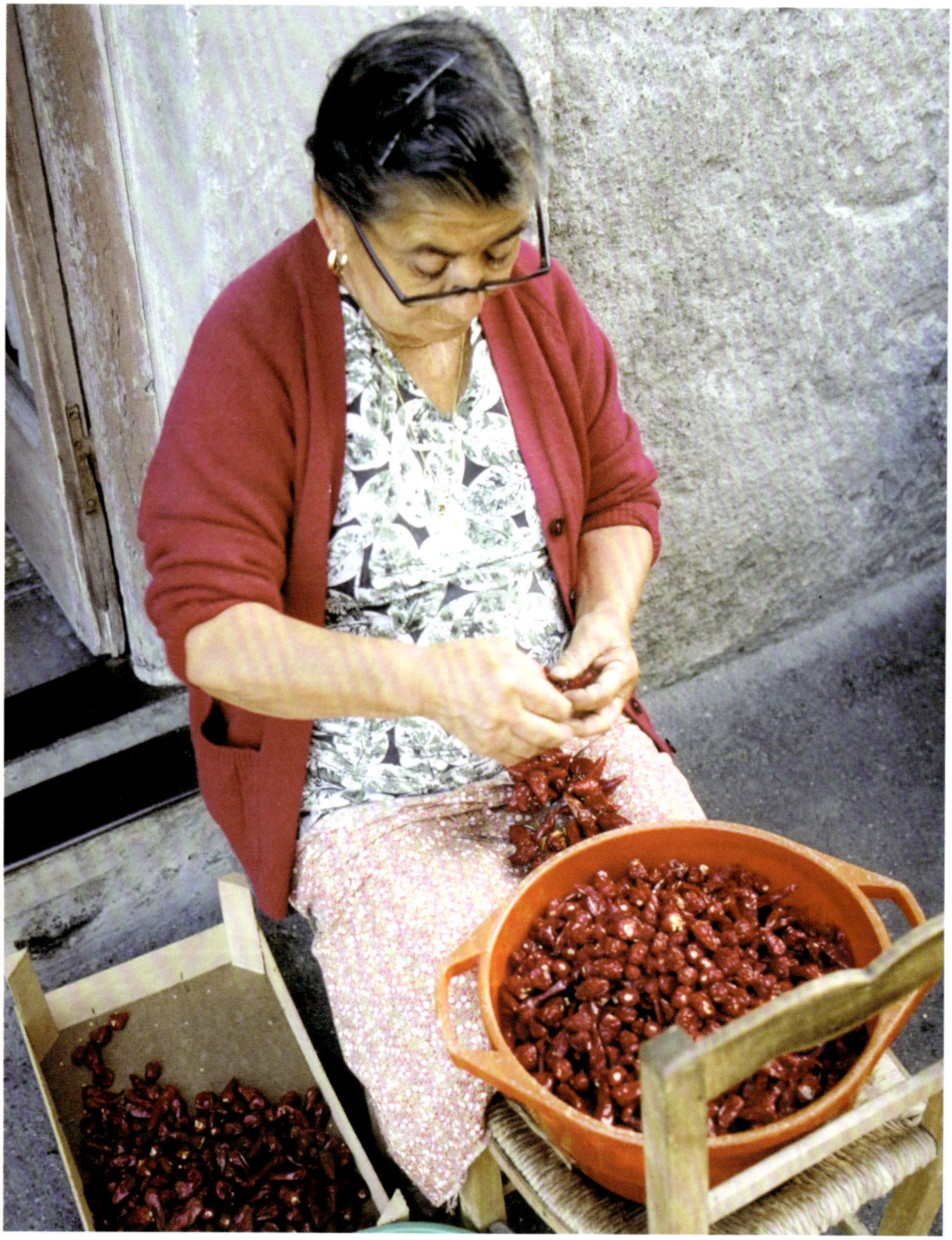

A woman may supplement her family's income with work she can do at home.

get out and vote. But even more than that, women must become actively involved in politics in their communities and must run for office. After all, it's difficult to elect women leaders when there are no women on the ballot.

WOMEN IN THE FAMILY

When people think of a woman's role in the family, they often think of a woman cooking, cleaning, and balancing a baby on her hip. Women's importance within families, however, goes far beyond these responsibilities. One of the most important functions women have always performed within their families and society is cultural transmission, or the passing on of beliefs, values, family history, and cultural practices from one generation to the next.

In many ways, cultural transmission is more important in the Mediterranean now than it has ever been before. In the Balkans, Mediterranean Asia, and Mediterranean North Africa, many people's lives have been disrupted by years of war, political disputes, and ethnic conflict. Some communities have faced ***genocide***. In some places, people fleeing persecution continue to live in refugee camps in other countries. The vast majority of refugees are women and children. Life in refugee camps is extremely unsettled and often important cultural practices cannot be maintained in the high-stress environment. Wars and conflicts also rob communities of their men, leaving women solely responsible for their families' and communities' survival.

Development and destruction of the environment also threatens the survival of certain Mediterranean cultures. ***Nomadic*** groups were once common in parts of the Mediterranean, but today most have been forced to abandon their way of life and live in settled communities. Many people who rely on agriculture also find their way of life threatened as rising populations, urban development, and poor environmental management take their toll. In situations like these, the role of cultural transmission that women have traditionally played is more important than ever to the continued survival of communities. This is not to say, however, that men do not also play an important and increasingly indispensable role in cultural transmission—but it is generally women who manage the household and spend the most time with the children. It is, therefore, women who often have the greatest influence on the next generation.

In some parts of the Mediterranean, family structure is very similar to what you are accustomed to in North America. In much of Mediterranean Europe, only the immediate family lives in a single dwelling, children move out on their own before getting married, marriage generally occurs well after the teen years, and people choose their own marriage partners with love as a number-one criterion. In other parts of the Mediterranean, however, family structure is very different from what we are used to in North America. Extended families continue to live together in one house, patrilocal community structures remain common, and marriage occurs relatively young (though no longer in the early teens as was once common). Having the extended family living in one house can be cramped but also very useful. In many areas, even women who don't want to work outside the home have no choice but to get a job to make ends meet. Services that can ease women's double burden of work and home/childcare, like daycare and after school programs, are scarce in much of the Mediterranean. With both parents working and with few options for affordable childcare, a grandparent in the home fills the needed role of childcare provider.

Arranged marriage continues to be common in some parts of the Balkans, Mediterranean Asia, and North Africa. In such places, many women want more control over marriage, not necessarily so that they can have a romantic, Western-style courtship, but so they can at least know the man and assess his qualities. But this desire to have a bit of control in the marriage process is often interpreted by families as a sign of rebellion, rejection, and disloyalty. "Why," parents might ask, "won't our daughter trust us to choose a suitable husband for her? Doesn't she trust our judgment? Doesn't she understand that we would

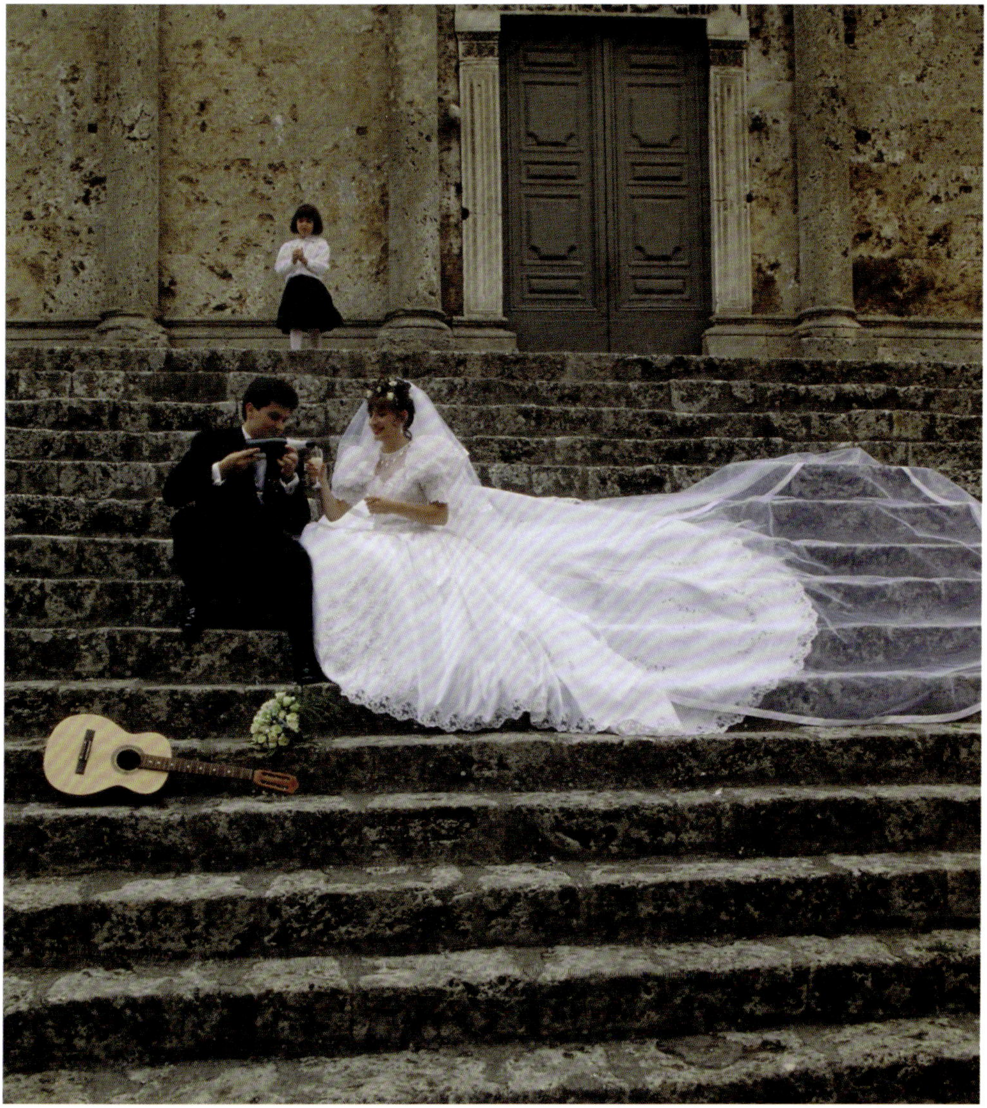

This modern Greek wedding is not typical of traditional Mediterranean marriage ceremonies.

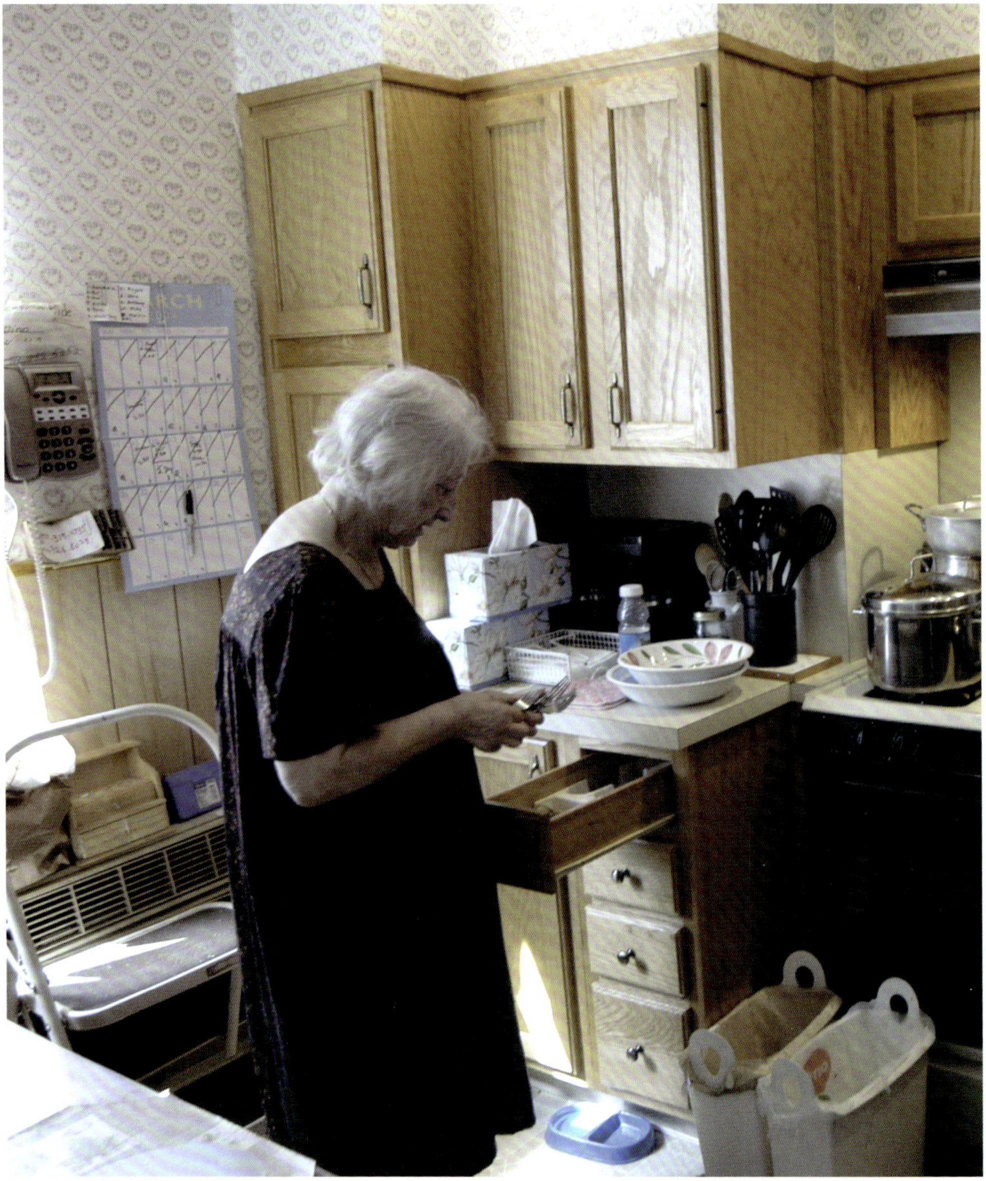

Many older Mediterranean women continue to live more traditional lives that focus on home and family.

only do what is in her best interest and in the best interest of the family?" But as women who want more of a say in marriage point out, sometimes what is in the best interest of the family is not in her best interest as an individual. This belief, however, is strictly at odds with the belief that what is in the best interest of the family is always the same as what is in the best interest for the individual.

Some people throughout Mediterranean Europe, Asia, and North Africa believe that family values have declined in recent decades. Whether this is actually the case is not as important as the fact that a perceived decline in morals and increase in crime are blamed largely on women's absence from the home. The belief is that women's absence from the home leads children to grow up without proper behavior and morals. Some people think that if women stayed home to raise their children, the whole society would improve. These beliefs are often held by both men and women. Such beliefs are also closely linked to religious values. Religion is important to most Mediterranean people, and religious traditions have a significant impact on society and women's lives.

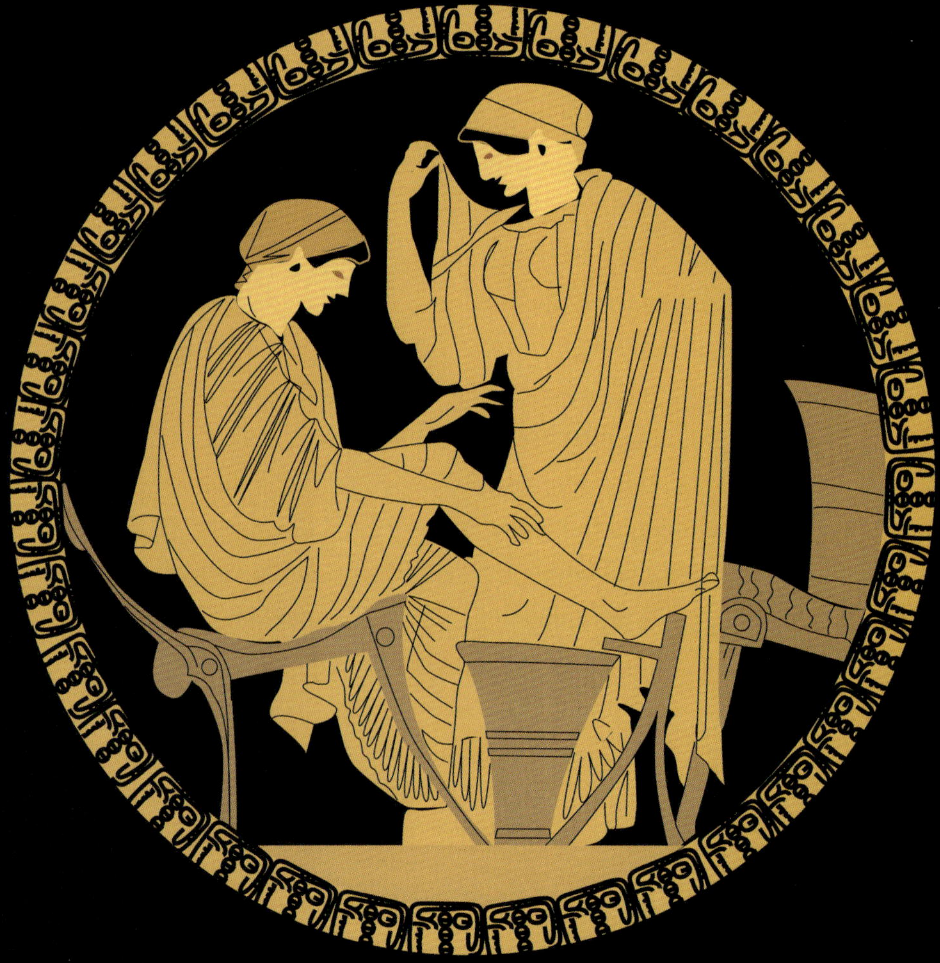

"WHAT WE REQUIRE IS NOT A FORMAL RETURN TO
TRADITION AND RELIGION, BUT A REREADING,
A REINTERPRETATION, OF OUR HISTORY THAT CAN ILLUMINATE
THE PRESENT AND PAVE THE WAY TO A BETTER FUTURE."
—NAWAL EL SAADAWI

4

RELIGIOUS INFLUENCES ON WOMEN'S LIVES

For centuries she has been called a prostitute, an adulteress, and a repentant sinner. Some have used her as a metaphor for all of womankind—a lowly creature tarnished by sex and vileness, whose only hope of redemption lies in acknowledging and forever denouncing her weak, pathetic, and filthy nature. But who was Mary Magdalene really? Was she truly the lowly prostitute that the Christian church has for centuries claimed, or was there much more to this woman's story? If she was more to the early Christian tradition than has previously been acknowledged, what does that mean for Christian women, and perhaps all religious women, today?

Until recently, Mary Magdalene has been best known in Christian communities as a prostitute who anointed Jesus' feet with perfume and received his forgiveness and blessing. According to scholars, like Karen L. King of Harvard Divinity School, recent archeological findings coupled with close examinations of existing biblical sources have revealed that this portrayal of Mary Magdalene is a complete myth. Nothing in Christian scriptures equates Mary Magdalene with another story about an unnamed prostitute, and instead, there is much evidence that Mary Magdalene played an extremely important role in the founding of the Christian Church. In fact, she is sometimes referred to as "the apostle to the apostles," for she was, according to scripture, the first to meet the resurrected Christ at his tomb and receive instruction from him. (Christians believe that Christ died to save human beings from their sins and then rose from the dead.)

Many scholars now believe that Mary Magdalene not only followed Jesus' teachings, but that she was one of a handful of women who financially supported Jesus, was one of his closest disciples, and was one of many female apostles who have been erased from the pages of history. In years to come, scholarship concerning this Mediterranean woman may teach us new things about women's importance in world religions, how that importance has been downplayed over time, and how knowledge of women's true religious past could transform practices today.

Today, as in Mary Magdalene's time, religion plays a central role in many Mediterranean people's lives. Christianity, Islam, and Judaism are the most influential of the region's religions. All of these religions have their origins in the Mediterranean world, and the beliefs associated with these religions affect women's lives in specific ways.

When considering religion's effects on women's lives, it is important to understand that religious approaches toward life are generally very different from ***secular*** approaches. Religions tend to be community oriented and far less ***individualistic*** than secular society. Individuals are expected to put the community before themselves and to put their god before all other things. Religions, therefore, believe that all people have certain duties to their god and to each other, and that obedience to the god's laws and fulfillment of all duties is necessary for the individual's and community's continued physical, mental, and spiritual well-being. This focus on an individual's duties is different from current secular

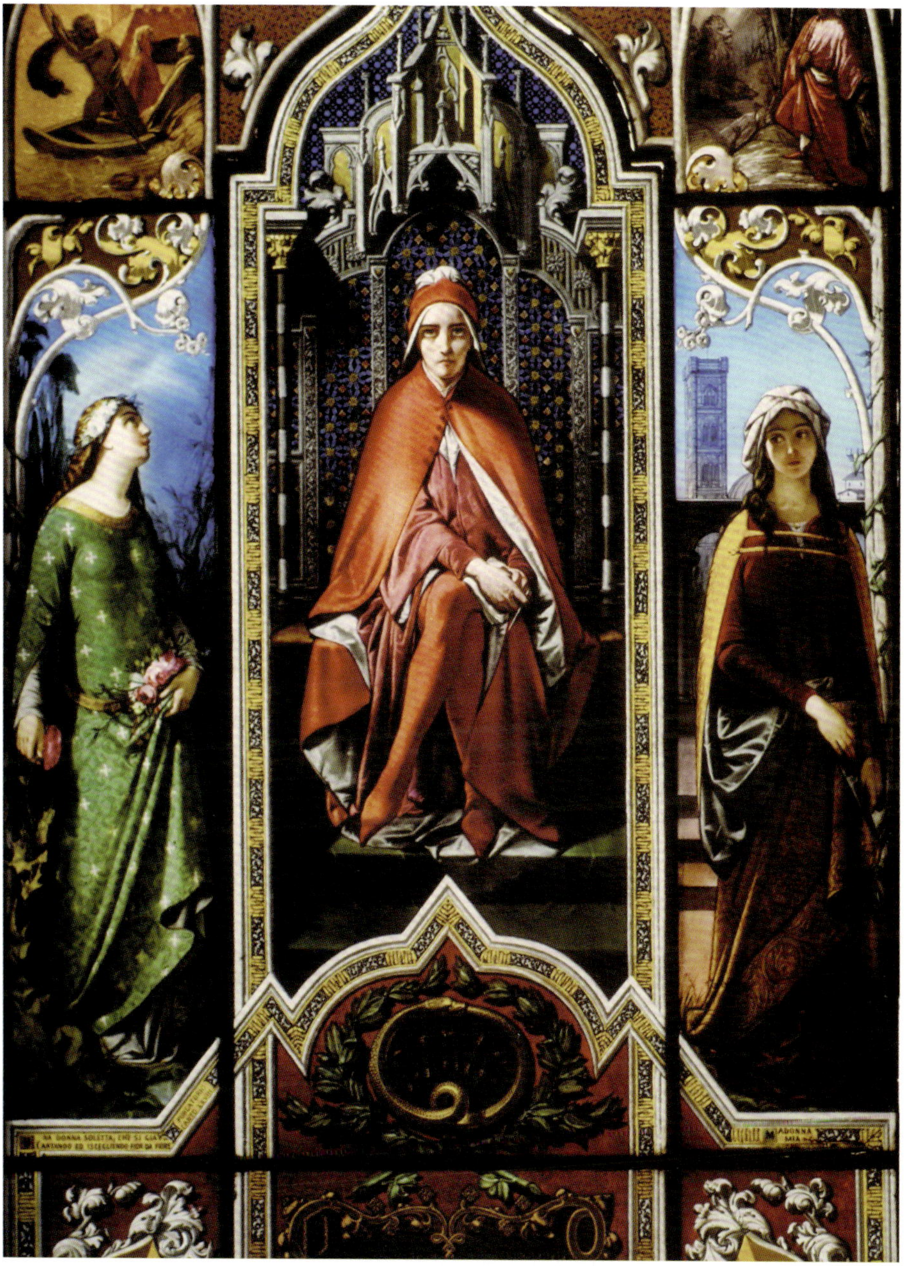

Religion plays an important role in the lives of Mediterranean women.

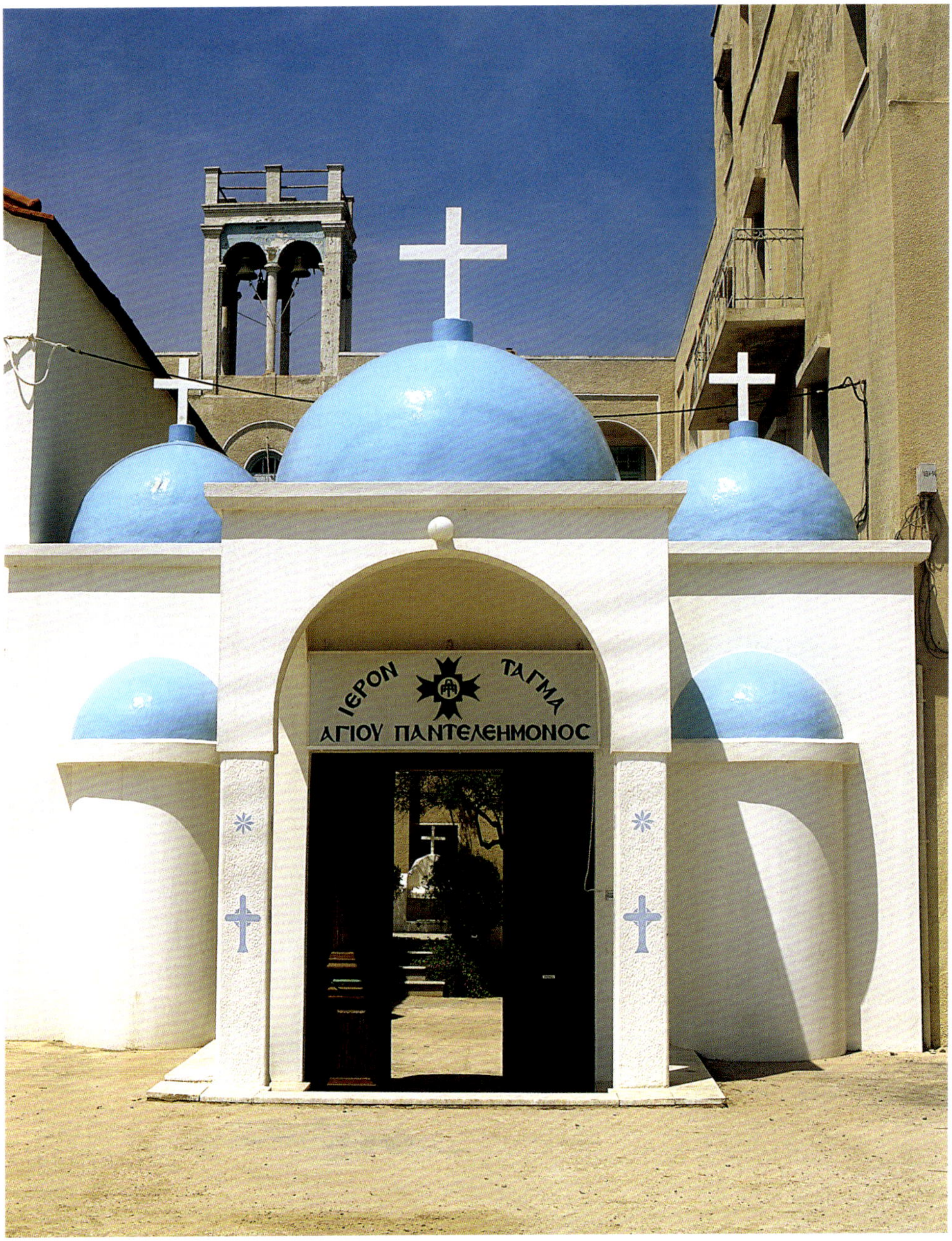

A Greek Orthodox church.

attitudes, which tend to focus on individuals' rights. For example, when a person examines her life through nonreligious eyes, she might likely ask, "Am I achieving everything that my rights entitle me to?" Examining her life through religious eyes, however, she might rather ask, "Am I fulfilling all of my duties to God and to my community?"

Christianity, Islam, and Judaism all believe that men and women have different duties and obligations that they are commanded by God to perform. If everyone fulfills his or her duties, the community will prosper, individuals will feel a spiritual closeness to God, and natural happiness will result. If an individual does not perform his or her duties, spiritual illness will lead to unhappiness, and the community may suffer. All of these religions have traditionally believed that a woman's religious duty and path to spiritual fulfillment lies in the home through being a good wife and mother. The religious texts of these religions (books like the Bible, ***Torah***, and ***Qur'an***) all equate the relationship between mother and child with the relationship between God and humans. Judaism and Islam especially emphasize the home as the center of spiritual life and elevate the role of mother as the highest female spiritual aspiration. In Christianity, although a religious home life is extremely important, the church is the focus of religious life, and dedicating one's life to the church by, for instance, becoming a nun, is also an option for women. This too is considered a marriage of sorts, as nuns are often referred to as "married to God." Though nuns are highly revered by their religions, they do not have the same status as priests (the male leaders of the church) and do not occupy the same leadership positions in the community.

In all three of these religions, a woman has specific religious duties and obligations that are different from those of a man. She has a duty to raise her children according to religious teachings and to support and obey her husband. In Judaism, there are three special commandments for women—the lighting of the candles for certain religious events or ceremonies, the separating of a portion of dough to be burned when making bread, and the taking of a ritual bath after menstruation has ended. In Islam, women are required to wear specific clothing that covers everything but the face and hands, is loose fitting so as not to reveal the shape of the body, is ***opaque***, and does not draw attention. In Orthodox Christianity, women must wear a head covering to church. These are just a few examples of religious requirements that are specific to women.

Though these religions stress marriage and motherhood as among the highest and most acceptable roles for women, none of them specifically forbid women from pursuing education or employment outside the home. In fact, each recognizes that a certain amount of education is necessary for a woman to understand her religion, serve God, and raise her children with a proper understanding of their faith. To the extent that it serves the community and God, these religions encourage education for women. However, these religions also discourage higher education and employment for women if it will detract from their primary roles as wives and mothers.

What if a woman does not want to be a wife and mother? Is she not fulfilling her religious duty, and are there no other options available to her if she wants to lead a religious life? This is a controversial topic upon which even members of the same religion cannot agree. In general, however, one could say that a woman's options to choose a life path other than wife and mother that is still in keeping with her religion's ideas of social and spiritual duty are limited. As we have said, in Christianity a woman can become a nun, but she is barred from becoming a priest or serving in the traditionally male leadership roles. Judaism and Islam also bar women from serving in the male leadership roles. Though a woman might be able to find a path for herself performing valued spiritual work in her community, there is no officially sanctioned spiritual occupation to which she can aspire.

Religions are variable, however. They change from place to place and over time. Christianity, for instance, has many different forms (the most common in

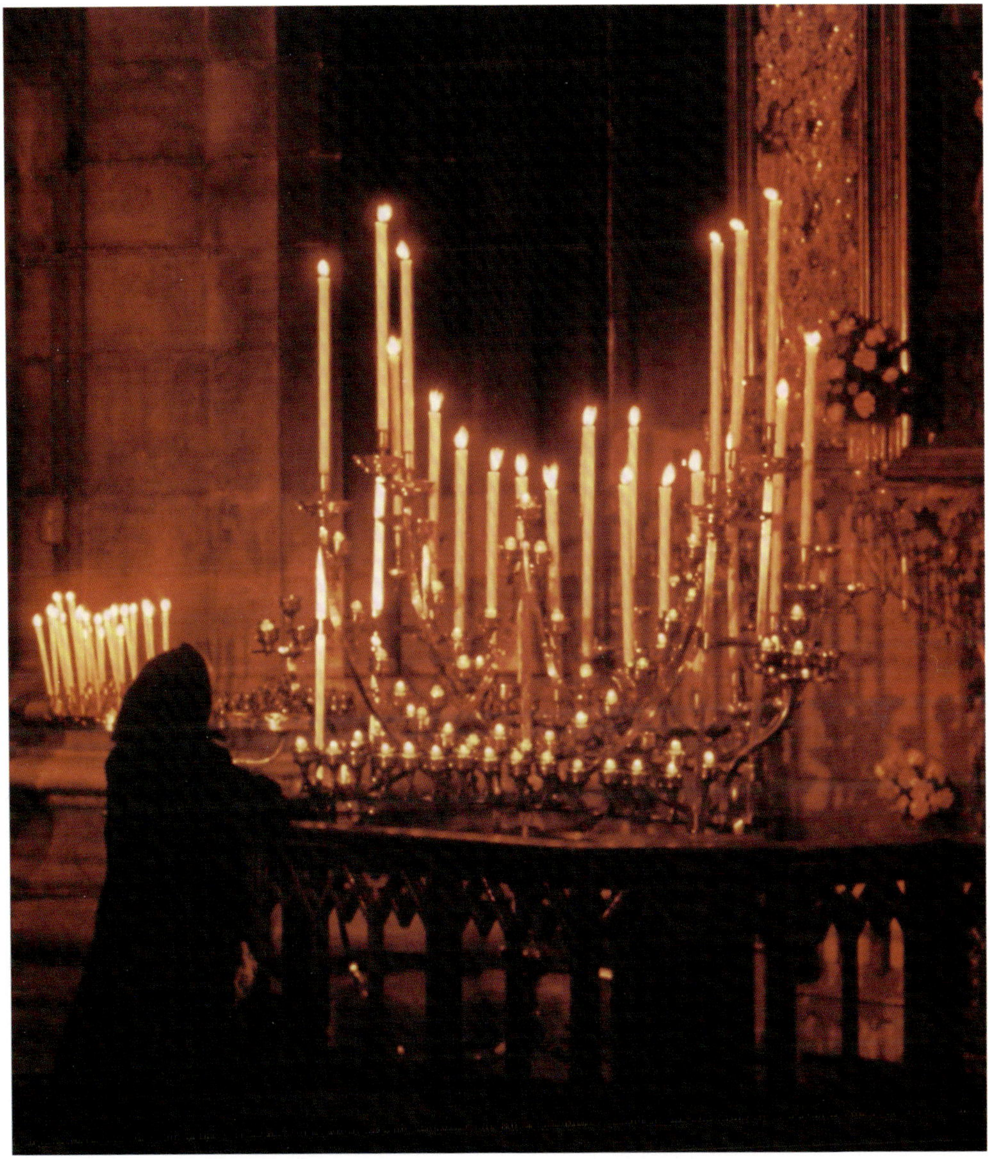

In Orthodox Christianity, women must wear head coverings in the church.

the Mediterranean are the Roman Catholic Church and the Eastern Orthodox Church), and the teachings of Christian traditions can be vastly different. Judaism and Islam also vary in their practices. All these religions incorporate traditions and texts that originated thousands of years ago, so it is impossible to know exactly what the original founders of these religions intended. Instead, religious communities have relied on generations of teachers, prophets, and religious scholars to interpret God's laws and words. These people did not always agree, especially when it came to religious teachings concerning women. Today, you will find some religious communities treating women with a great deal of equality, while other communities that claim to be of the same religion treat

"No nation can rise to the height of glory unless your women are side by side with you; we are victims of evil customs. It is a crime against humanity that our women are shut up within four walls of the houses as prisoners. There is not sanction anywhere for the deplorable condition in which our women have to live."
—Allama Muhammad Iqbal, Islamic scholar, philosopher, and poet.

women as inferior beings and regulate everything about their lives. Both communities will claim that Scripture instructs them to treat women as they do, and yet they treat women in completely different ways.

In recent decades, ***fundamentalist*** religions have received especially strong condemnation by outside groups for their maltreatment of women and use of religious scriptures as an excuse for such maltreatment. Groups that are oppressive to women, however, are not necessarily following their religion's true teachings. Today, Islamic fundamentalist groups are some of the highest profile religious organizations in the world, but their activities are by no means characteristic of Muslim society and teachings.

FUNDAMENTALIST RELIGION

In some areas of the Mediterranean today where fundamentalist religions are practiced, women are confined to their homes, forbidden to speak to men who are not members of their families, denied an education, required to cover their faces in public, and severely punished, even killed, for the most minor of ***transgressions***.

In many ways, fundamentalism is a response to changing global conditions. In today's world of global economies, worldwide communication systems, new technologies, and increased international contact, it is becoming more difficult for many people to maintain their traditional ways of life. People see their children learning values from television, movies, magazines, and other sources, and sometimes these values contrast with their own beliefs. They see family members moving to cities for better-paying jobs. They see old ways of life sloughed off as new practices are adopted. What some people see as great opportunities in today's world are for other people a cultural onslaught that threatens to destroy their long-held way of life. Some people respond to these changing conditions by increasing their focus on customs and traditions and limiting their community's or family's access to anything that threatens their beliefs.

Fundamentalism often results in attempts to confine women to home- and family-oriented roles. Many people claim that they are preserving women's traditional roles. People who believe that too many Western values are being adopted and that individual cultures are being eroded may claim that confining women to "traditional" roles is necessary for the continued survival of their people and way of life, but in some cases these "traditional roles" are in reality more restrictive than the roles women have historically had.

Religion and Women's Reproductive Rights

Religion also plays a key role in women's approach to family planning. Many people consider a woman's ability to control her reproduction to be a fundamental part of her rights to equality and ***self-determination***. Many religions, on the other hand, see attempts to control the reproductive process as interference with God's will. In the Mediterranean and around the world today, one of the most discussed topics relating to women's issues is access to abortion and multiple methods of birth control. Few issues in the world are as controversial and as ***polarizing*** as that of abortion, but abortion has also been a central issue in worldwide movements for women's rights and is inevitably part of discussing religion's effect on women's lives.

Today, abortion is widely available in Mediterranean Europe, but continues to be largely restricted in Mediterranean Asia and North Africa. Women's access to birth control and abortion, however, is greatly affected by local circumstances, like the beliefs of the religious community in which she lives. Even if abortion and contraception are legal and available within a country, religious beliefs and cultural practices still may bar a woman from using these forms of birth control.

What determines whether or not abortion is permissible from a religious perspective depends on when human life is thought to begin. None of the religions, however, agree on when this occurs. In Judaism, it is traditionally

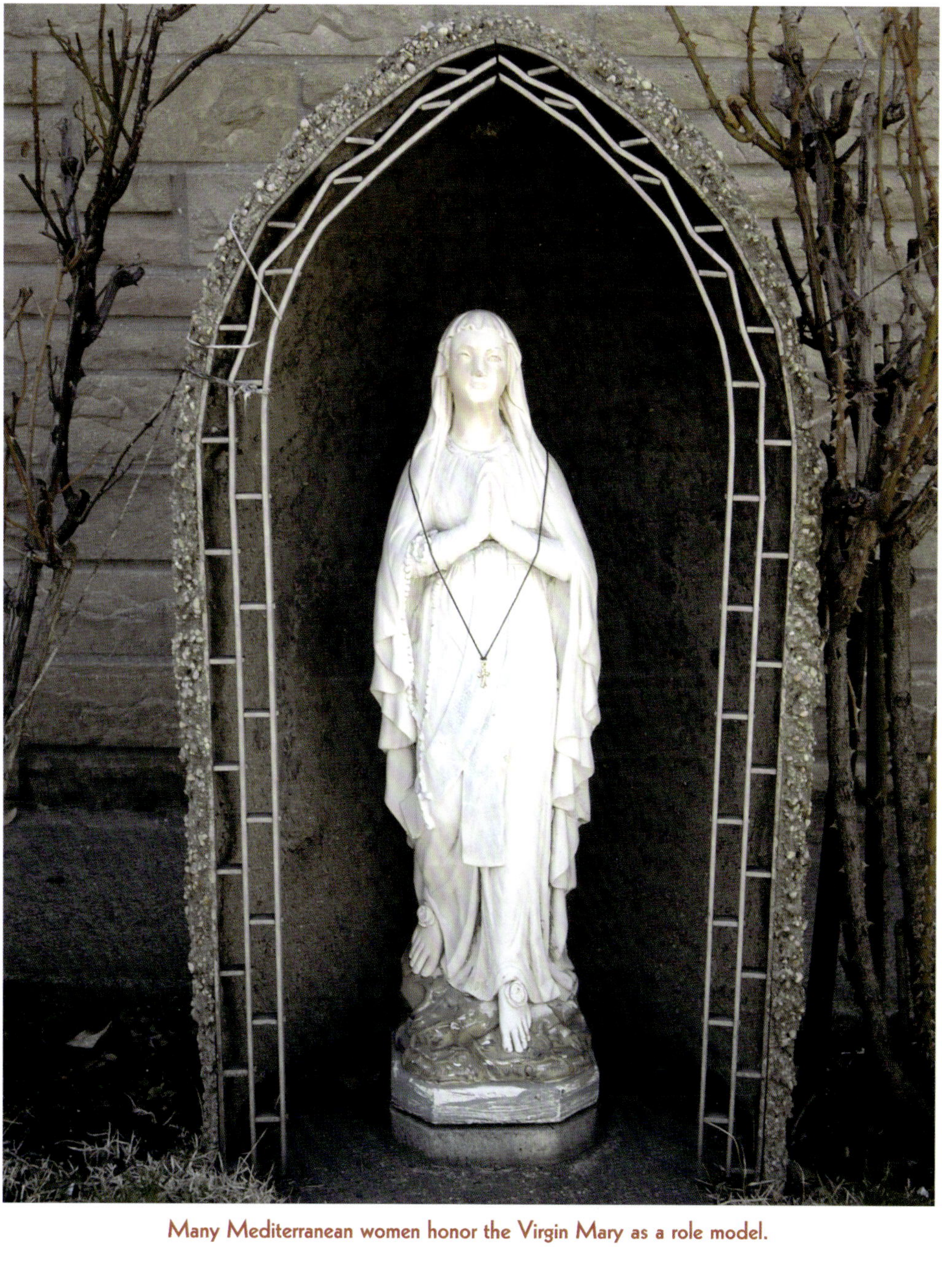

Many Mediterranean women honor the Virgin Mary as a role model.

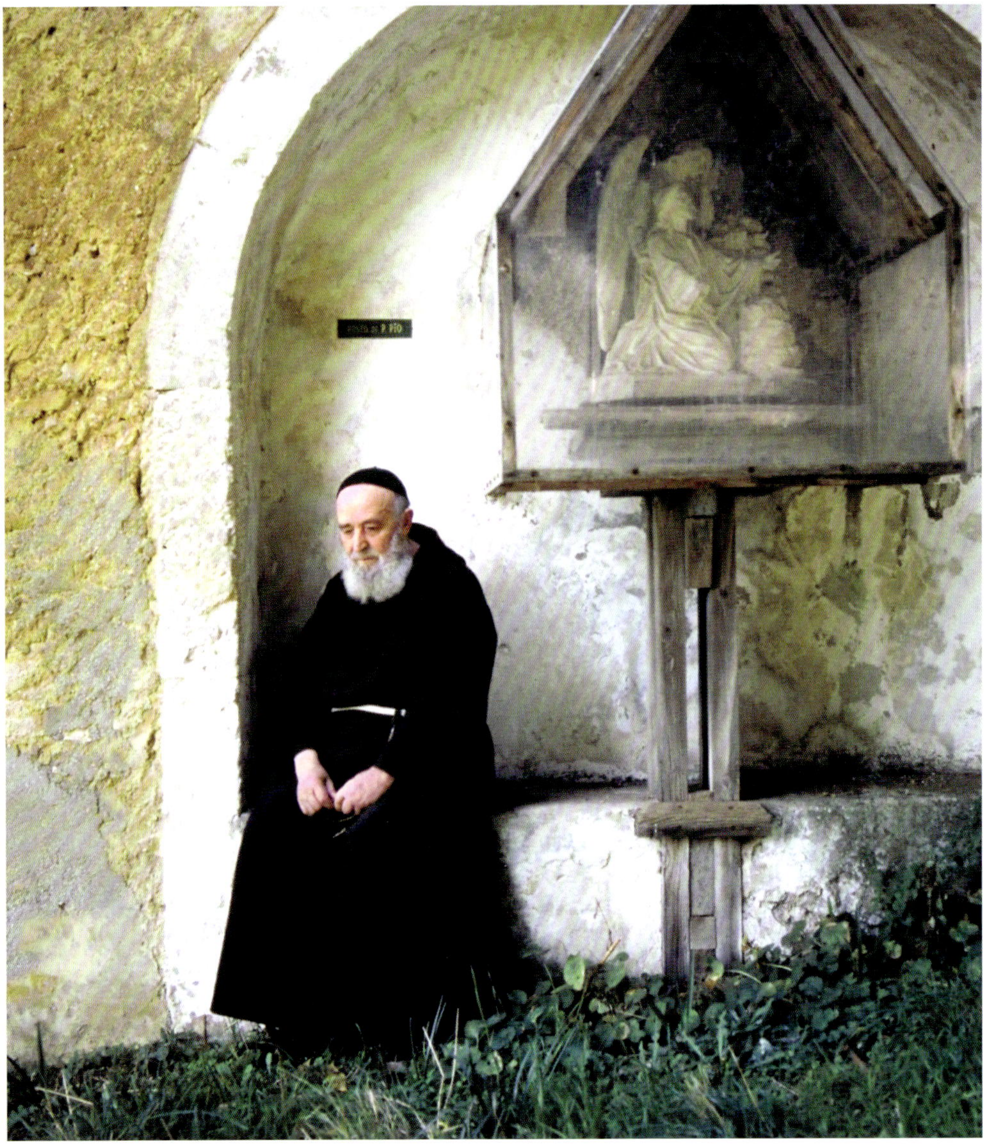

The teachings of male religious leaders often shape the lives of Mediterranean women.

believed that a fetus becomes a full human being when the head emerges from the womb. In Judaism, abortion (though not encouraged) is generally accepted if performed for appropriate reasons, such as danger to the mother's life. Certain forms of female birth control, such as "the pill," are generally accepted as well if pregnancy is being avoided for the appropriate reasons, but forms of male birth control that interrupt the passage of sperm (like condoms) are generally not permitted.

In Islamic belief, the child is believed to become a human being somewhat earlier than in Jewish belief. The soul is thought to have entered the child by the fourth month of pregnancy. Therefore, abortion is not permissible after this time. In some Islamic groups, abortion is not permissible at all, but in most forms of Islam, abortion can be performed until the fortieth or the 120th day of pregnancy (again, if performed for accepted reasons). If used for the correct purposes, birth control is also generally permitted by Islamic law.

In Christianity, the soul is believed to enter the child at the moment of conception, and abortion is therefore never acceptable. The Roman Catholic Church tends to be the most strict when it comes to abortion and contraception. Contraception is also generally not acceptable, as it is considered to interfere with God's will and to remove God's procreative purpose from sex. The Roman Catholic Church is opposed to all "artificial" forms of birth control. According to the church, any substance (like the birth control pill) or object (like condoms) that interferes with the body's natural reproductive processes is considered "artificial."

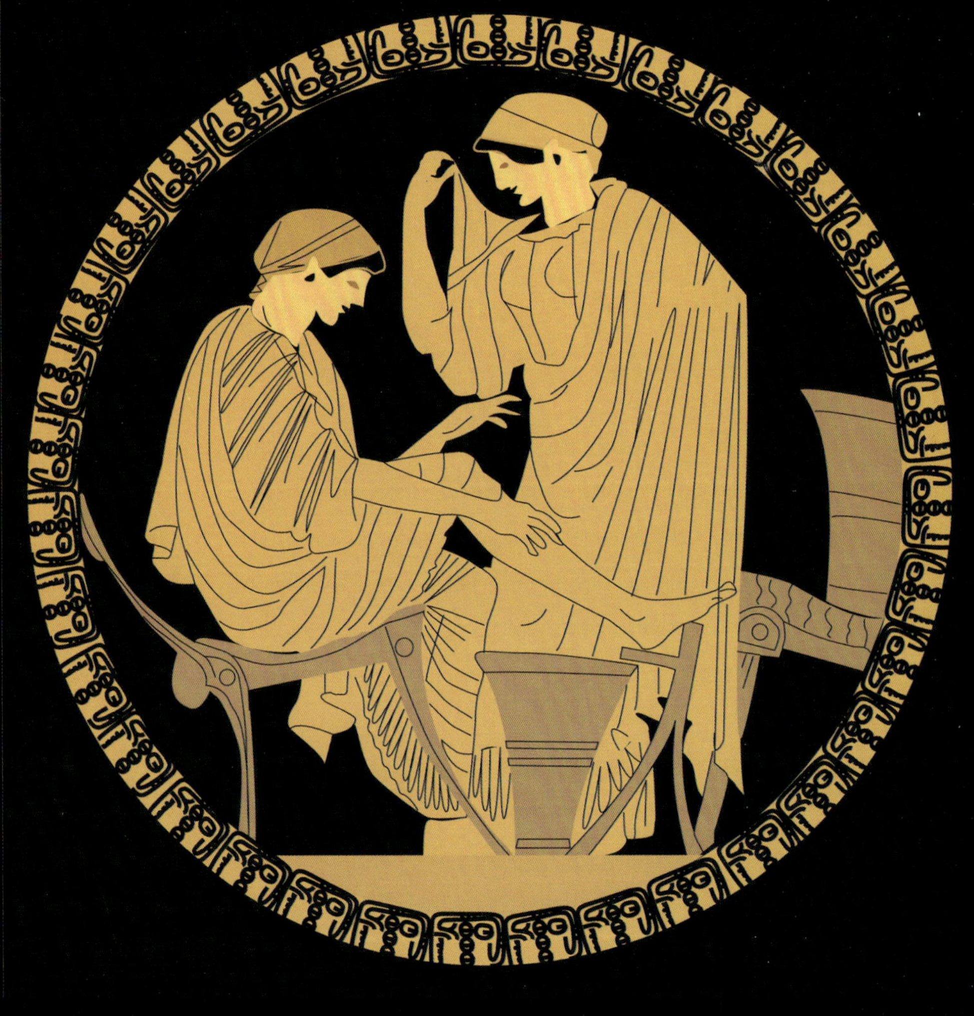

"WELL-BEHAVED WOMEN RARELY MAKE HISTORY."
—LAUREL THATCHER ULRICH

5

THE STUFF OF MYTHS AND LEGENDS: POWERFUL MEDITERRANEAN WOMEN OF THE PAST

As we have seen in previous chapters, women have long held a subservient role in Mediterranean society that afforded them few opportunities outside of their roles as wives and mothers. Nevertheless, throughout the ages, some women have risen to positions of influence and power. Here are just a few stories of real Mediterranean women who created a stir in their own time and continue to fascinate us today.

HATSHEPSUT OF EGYPT

Hatshepsut's reign began in 1490 B.C.E. in the age of the Egyptian Pharaohs. Hatshepsut was the daughter of the reigning Pharaoh, Tuthmose I. Some evidence suggests that Hatshepsut was Tuthmose's favorite child, but she was female so she could not inherit the throne. When the Pharaoh died, his son Tuthmose II rose to the throne.

In Ancient Egypt, royalty often married their close relatives. Hatshepsut and Tuthmose II were half-siblings (they had different mothers but the same father), but were nevertheless married. Tuthmose II was sickly, while Hatshepsut

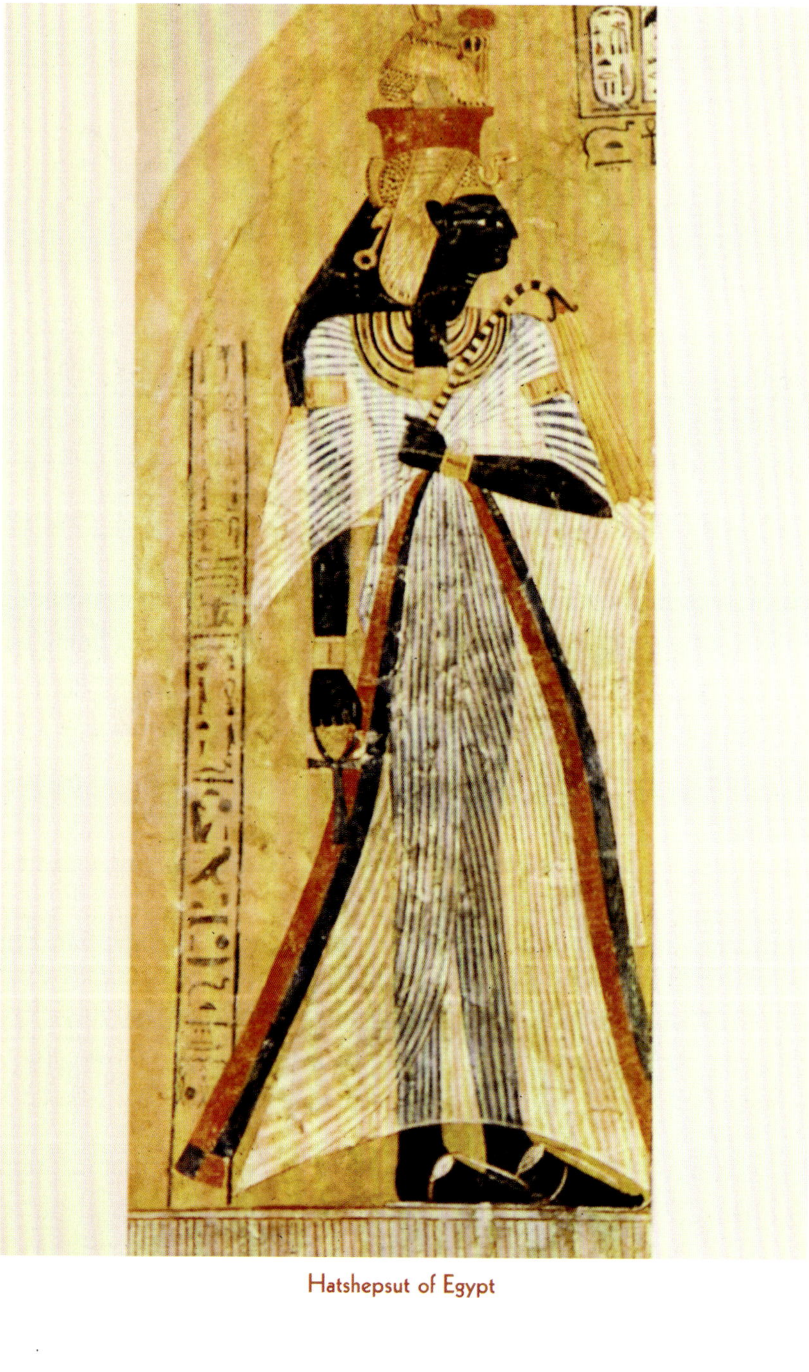

Hatshepsut of Egypt

had a talent for politics, diplomacy, and matters of state. Hatshepsut quickly became the power behind the scenes. During this time, she gave birth to a daughter by another man, and Tuthmose II fathered a son, Tuthmose III, by another woman. When, after less than five years of rule, Tuthmose II died, his son was in line to inherit the throne. Since Tuthmose III was so young, however, Hatshepsut was permitted to continue deciding the affairs of state as ***regent*** to the young king.

Hatshepsut, however, was popular among the priests and powerful men of Egypt, and soon she made the bold move of declaring herself the "Female King of Egypt." She had enough support to secure her position, so she donned the traditional clothing, headcloth, and false beard of the King and pushed her nephew aside. Then she embarked on what would be a successful twenty years of rule.

Unlike her predecessors whose reigns focused on military exploits, evidence suggests that Hatshepsut's reign was a visionary one of peace and prosperity. Instead of sending military units to conquer other lands, she sent expeditions in search of exotic animals, spices, trees, and other things the Egyptians valued. Hatshepsut erected stunning monuments and commissioned the building of a grand temple.

Historians are not certain how Hathsepsut died, though many speculate that her nephew, sick of being confined to the shadows, masterminded her demise. Whether her death was natural or murder, it seems that Tuthmose III had enough burning resentment for his aunt to order the desecration of her tomb, the disposal of her body, and the destruction of many of her works. As the new king, he had Hatshepsut's name removed from many records and replaced with his own, thus laying claim to many of Hatshepsut's works. The truth about this great Mediterranean woman's life continues to be uncovered today.

CLEOPATRA VII, THE "SERPENT OF THE NILE"

More than one thousand years after Hatshepsut's reign, Egypt's most famous female ruler came to power. Today, myths of Cleopatra VII are filled with tales of her bewitching beauty and powers of seduction. The little evidence remaining from her life, however, suggests that she was not at all beautiful and that looks had very little to do with her rise to power. So what did Cleopatra have?

Brains! Cleopatra was a brilliant young woman. She spoke at least nine languages and was a talented mathematician. She was also a keen observer of human nature, a shrewd politician, and a bit of an actress. She had the smarts to discern what role was needed, and then the ability to carry that role off, allowing her to be everything from intellectual to commoner, warrior to seductress, depending on her audience.

In Cleopatra's time, the Egyptian royal family was actually descended from the Macedonian Greeks who had seized the throne in 304 B.C.E. Cleopatra was the first and only one in this long line of rulers to learn the Egyptian language which her subjects spoke.

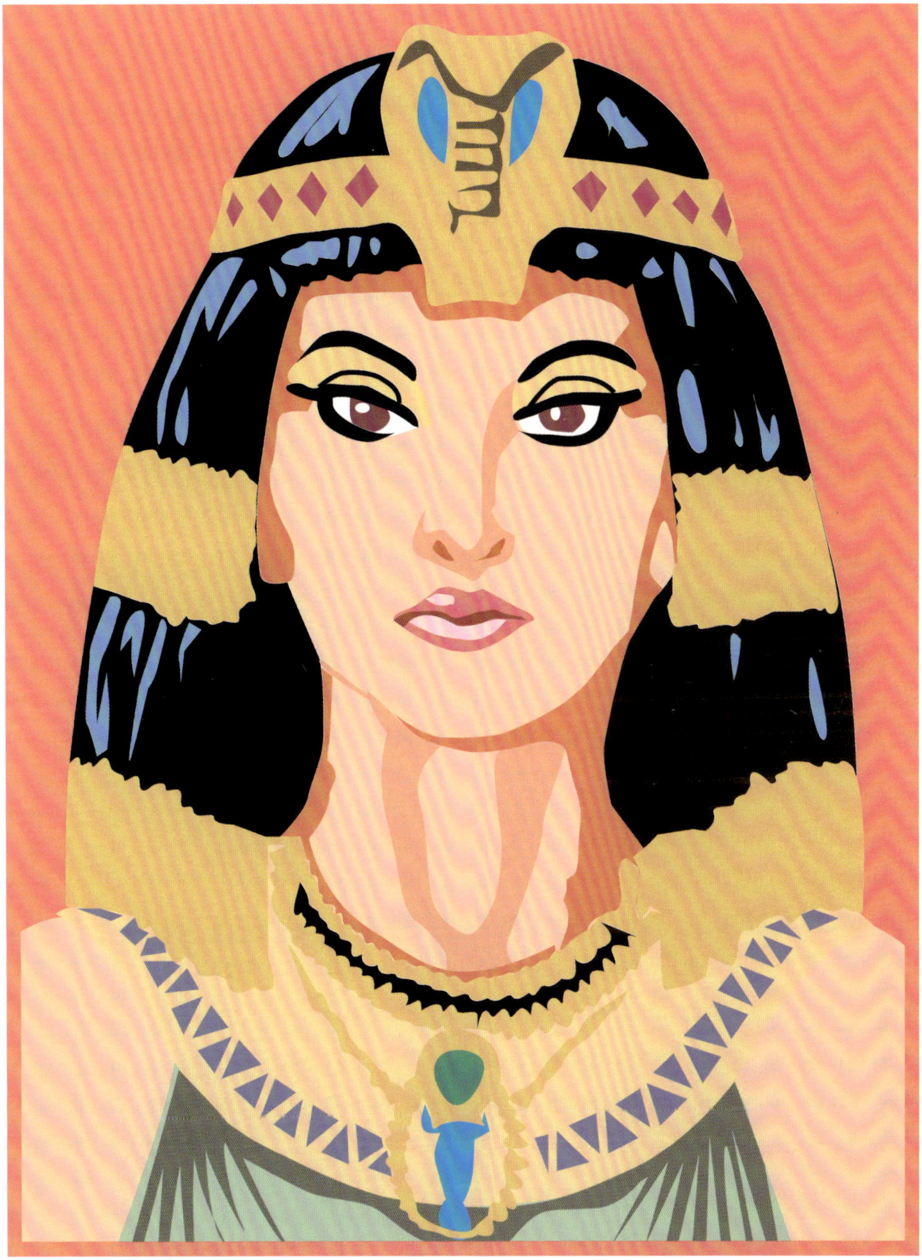

Cleopatra VII

Cleopatra was born in 69 B.C.E., a time when Egypt's influence in the Mediterranean was crumbling in the face of the advancing Roman Empire. Cleopatra was seventeen when her father died and passed Egypt's leadership on to her and her twelve-year-old brother, Ptolemy XIII. As was traditional for the royal family, Cleopatra married her brother. Like Hathsepsut of so many ages ago, however, she soon confined him to the shadows. This initiated a serious power struggle between Cleopatra and her supporters and those supporting Ptolemy. Cleopatra and her supporters were, for a time, driven from Alexandria (the Egyptian capital).

Cleopatra, however, would not remain in exile for long. The evidence we have today suggests that Cleopatra felt a great passion for Egypt and had ambitions to match. She wanted to see the whole of the Mediterranean united. And who would be at the head of this new empire? Well, she would, of course. To realize such goals, Cleopatra knew she would have to make an alliance with Rome, to whom the Egyptian government already owed money. The Roman leader, Julius Caesar, was in fact advancing on Egypt with the intent to collect. If an alliance was going to be made, it needed to be made fast!

There was just one problem. That pesky brother of hers had an army between Cleopatra and Julius Caesar.

Ptolemy happened to be away when Caesar arrived in Alexandria. Finding the palace empty of its rulers, Caesar boldly made himself at home. Before her brother could return, Cleopatra had herself rolled in a carpet and snuck past her enemies into Caesar's company. Her brother arrived the next day to find that Cleopatra and Caesar had already made both a personal and a political alliance. A war ensued in which Cleopatra and Caesar were victorious, and Ptolemy died fleeing Alexandria.

Cleopatra once again had control in Alexandria, but according to Egyptian law, a woman could not rule alone. To secure her leadership, Cleopatra married another brother, this time eleven-year-old Ptolemy XIV. Her loyalties, however, whether for love or for politics, were with Caesar. They soon had a son and went to live in Rome. Caesar, though popular among the people of Rome, was quickly losing popularity among many in Rome's government who thought he was too power hungry. Cleopatra's presence did not help. Caesar was already married, yet he unapologetically brought Cleopatra and their son into his home. To make matters worse, many people disliked Cleopatra for her foreign ways. It was not long before Caesar was assassinated, and Cleopatra, fearing for their lives, took her son and fled back to Egypt.

Cleopatra's quest for her own and Egypt's greatness, however, would not stop with this little setback. Upon her return, she found that many things in Egypt had fallen into disrepair in her absence. She quickly set about putting things back in order. Her reigning brother/husband mysteriously vanished from the public record at this time, fueling suspicions that Cleopatra had him assassinated. Whatever the cause for Ptolemy's disappearance, Cleopatra's son was soon on the throne. This was convenient. Since he was only four years old, Cleopatra could once again sidestep the laws against female rule, this time reigning in her son's name.

After Caesar's death, a triumvirate was established in Rome. One of these new rulers was a military leader named Mark Antony who took control of the eastern portion of the Roman Empire. Rather than behaving as a diminutive subject of Mark Antony's new lands, Cleopatra at first ignored him. Angered by Cleopatra's attitude, Antony demanded that the Egyptian leader meet with him and answer for her insubordination. Antony was probably expecting Cleopatra to crawl forward on bended knee the way so many of his other subjects did, but instead she obeyed his order in Cleopatra style. She sailed on a richly adorned, perfumed barge. Instead of alighting to meet Antony on his land, Cleopatra invited Antony to supper on her lavish stage. Once aboard, Antony was quickly caught up in Cleopatra's well-choreographed show. By the end of the visit, Cleopatra had made a new alliance with Rome.

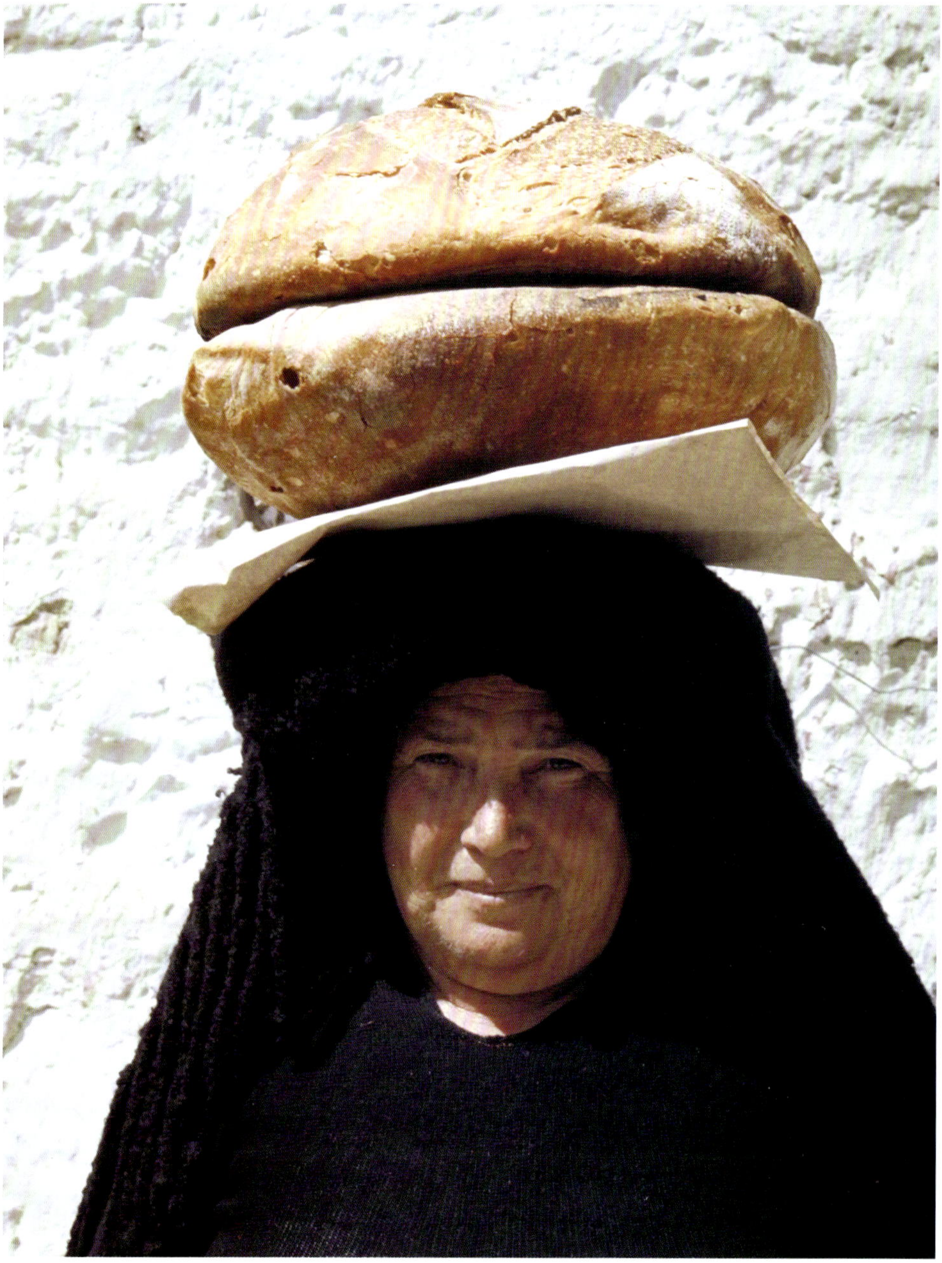

Most of today's Mediterranean women have far less power than Cleopatra!

MARY PROPHETISSA OF ALEXANDRIA

Not all the influential Mediterranean women made their mark in government. Mary Prophetissa of Alexandria, Egypt was influential through science and invention. She practiced alchemy, a partly scientific, partly spiritual field that was the precursor to today's chemistry. In her work, she invented the double boiler, built the first true still, and created the first lead/copper alloy—all things that we still use today.

Antony married Cleopatra despite having a wife in Rome. For the next decade, Cleopatra and Antony planned their great Mediterranean empire. They had three children and envisioned them as the next generation of great rulers. None of this, however, sat well with Rome, and soon Cleopatra and Antony were once again at war. This time, however, they would not be triumphant. Soon after losing an important battle, Antony committed suicide, and Cleopatra was captured. Rather than be walked through the streets of Rome and humiliated, as was the tradition for captives of war, Cleopatra had a poisonous snake smuggled to her and committed suicide by its bite. Thus Rome was denied its final triumph over Cleopatra, but it still had its final triumph over Egypt.

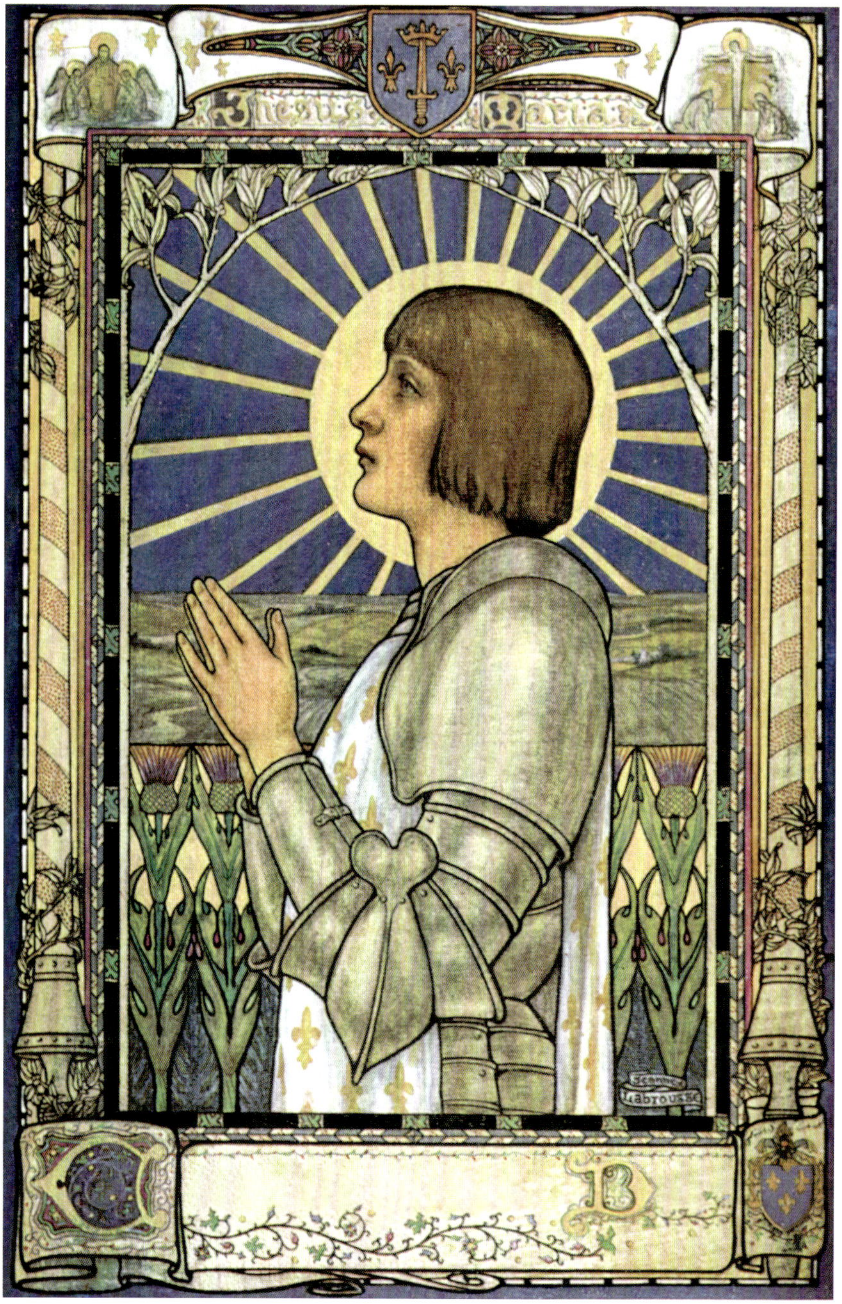

Joan of Arc

JOAN OF ARC

In the early 1400s, a teenage girl rose to be a French army captain, a powerfully spiritual leader, and a savior of her people. This girl's name was Joan of Arc. She was born to a farming family in the French countryside around 1412. At twelve years old, Joan began having visions and hearing voices that would direct her future and significantly impact the future of France.

Young Joan believed that the voices she heard belonged to the Catholic saints Michael, Catherine, and Margaret, and that their messages concerned England's attempts to seize France and its throne. England had invaded France when Joan was about three years old. With a weak army and resistance, there was little to drive England back. Charles, thought by many to be the legitimate heir to France's throne, had been denied his crown. The voices Joan heard, however, told her that she would be the force to overpower the English military, secure her country's sovereignty, and bring Charles to the throne. Following the voices' instructions, Joan donned a man's uniform, cut her hair, and sought a military appointment.

It took Joan a while to convince the future king and a group of theologians that God had indeed chosen her for a divine mission on behalf of her country. After weeks of examination, however, they were convinced that Joan was indeed a divinely touched soul. She was given a captainship and word spread that a saint was amongst the French troops. One might think that military men would be loath to follow a woman, but Joan touched something in the French army that no one else could rouse. She was armed only with a religious banner, but when Joan rode into battle with only her faith to protect her, the troops rallied with a renewed faith of their own. That spring Joan led them in their first victory against the English. What followed was a stunning sweep of victories as Joan's army marched across France reclaiming the besieged territories. It seemed that all Joan had to do was hold her banner high and call for the troops

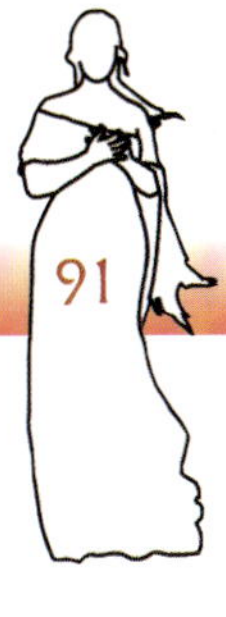

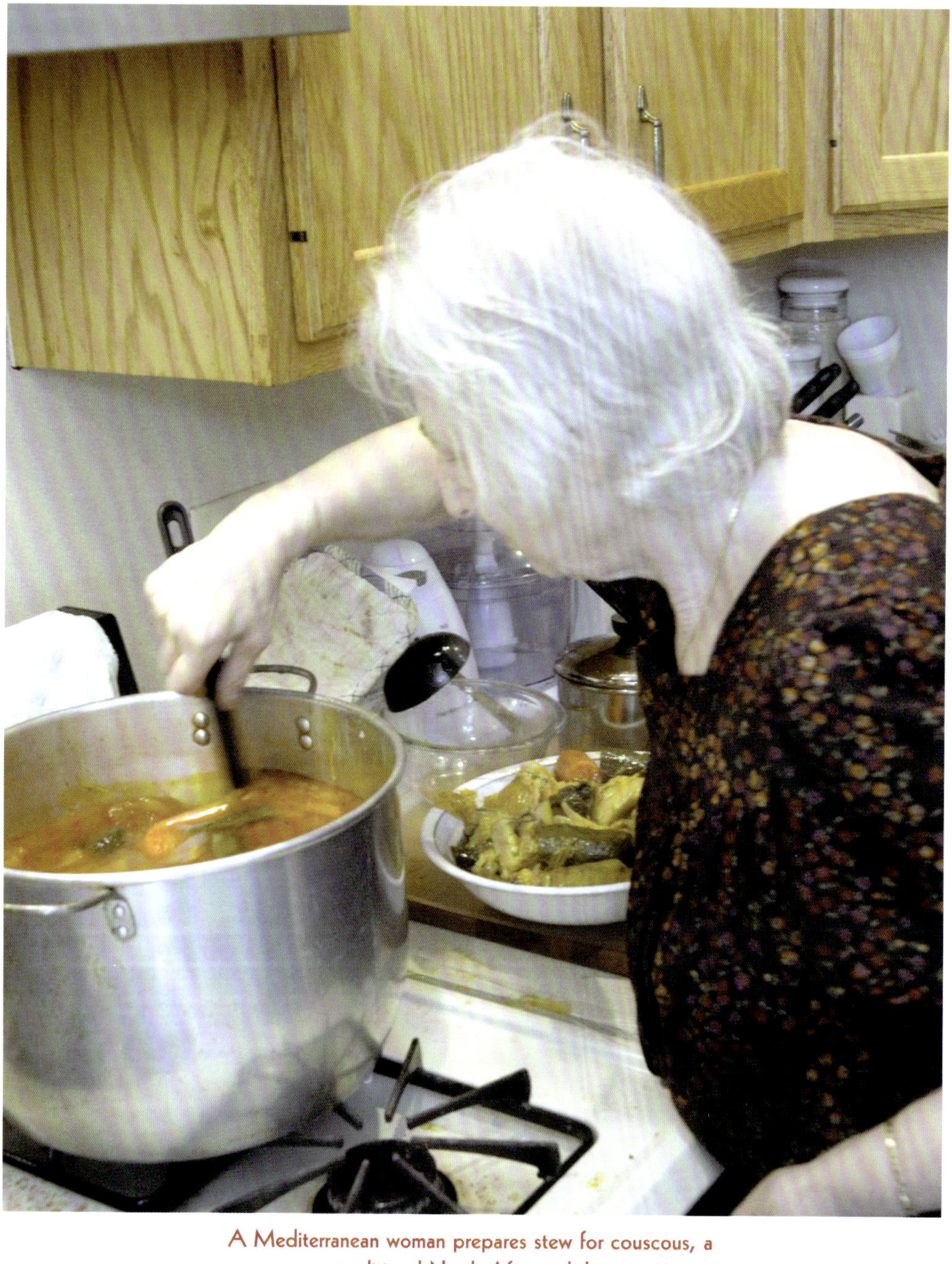

A Mediterranean woman prepares stew for couscous, a traditional North African dish.

to have courage, and the battle would be won. As her fame spread, some towns ceded without a fight. Soon Joan had led Charles to his throne and stood beside him as he was crowned king.

With the crowning of the new king, however, the tides turned for Joan. She set off to capture the remaining French territories under English control. Charles, now influenced by government advisors, began to go against Joan's military intuitions, something he had never done before. At one point, while she was wounded, he ordered her army disbanded. Over the next year, her forces shrank in size, support from the government and citizens slowed to a trickle, and plots and betrayals began. By the time Charles realized that he and many others were being manipulated by pro-English forces who had ***infiltrated*** the French government, it was already too late for Joan.

She was betrayed, captured, and turned over to the English. Accusing her of being a ***heretic***, the English embarked on a mockery of a trial. Corrupt from the beginning and designed as a way to get revenge upon the teenage girl who had led armies against them, the court eventually convicted Joan of heresy. For the crime of wearing men's clothing, something Joan did to protect herself from rape (women were often raped by soldiers and jailers, and men's clothing with its ties and laces offered much more protection than women's dresses), she was sentenced and burned at the stake. Joan of Arc was later pronounced innocent, proclaimed a martyr, and ***canonized*** as a saint, but the world had already lost one of the Mediterranean's greatest women.

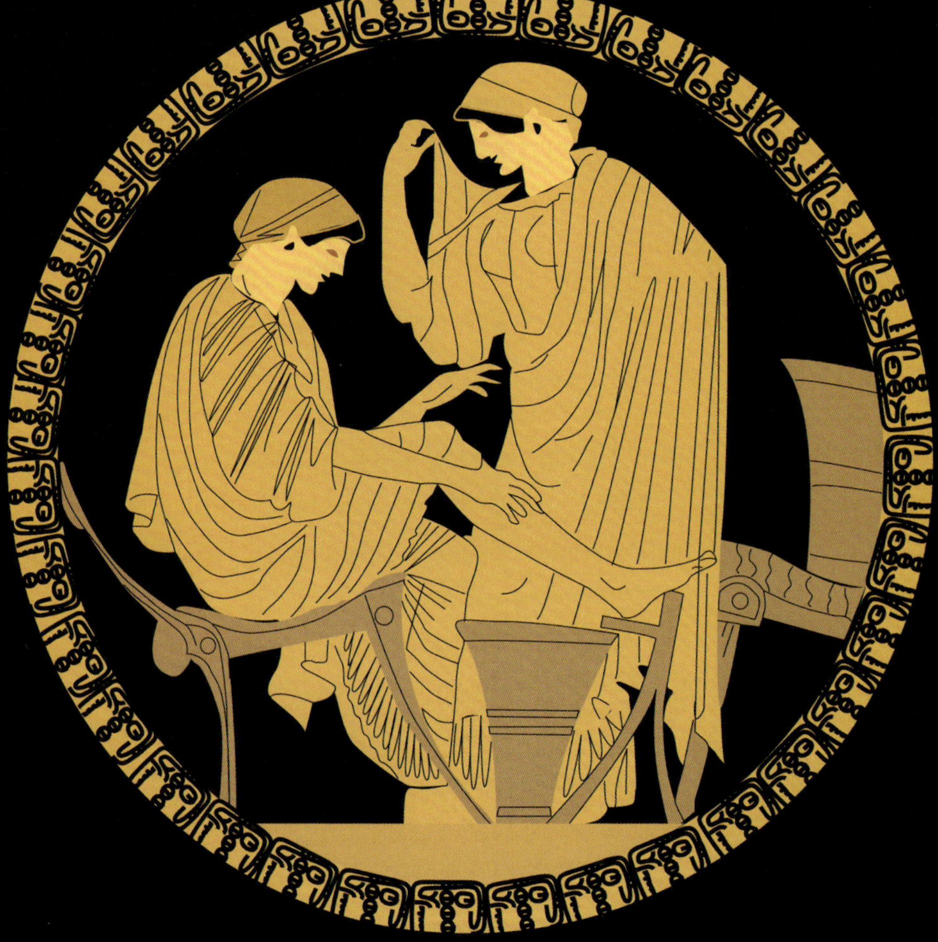

"[WOMEN] ARE A FUNDAMENTAL FORCE FOR LEADERSHIP, CONFLICT RESOLUTION AND THE PROMOTION OF LASTING PEACE AT ALL LEVELS."
—BEIJING DECLARATION, UNITED NATIONS, FOURTH WORLD CONFERENCE ON WOMEN

6

A NEW GENERATION OF INFLUENTIAL WOMEN

The tradition of influential Mediterranean women did not end in ancient times. In fact, even when incredibly restricted by their societies, women have always found ways to make great contributions to communities and civilization. That tradition continues to be alive and well today.

GOLDA MEIR

Born in Ukraine in 1898, Golda Meir was not a native of the Mediterranean region. In 1921, however, she immigrated to Palestine. In the following decades, she became one of the Mediterranean's most influential people of the twentieth century.

Although Golda Meir is in some ways a controversial figure, she is seen as a hero by the Jewish people of Israel and by many other people around the world. When Meir was born, her native Eastern Europe was an oppressive and dangerous place for Jewish people, and many fled their persecution and forced poverty. Meir's family immigrated to Milwaukee, Wisconsin, where she spent much of her young life before moving to Palestine. Once in Palestine, Meir

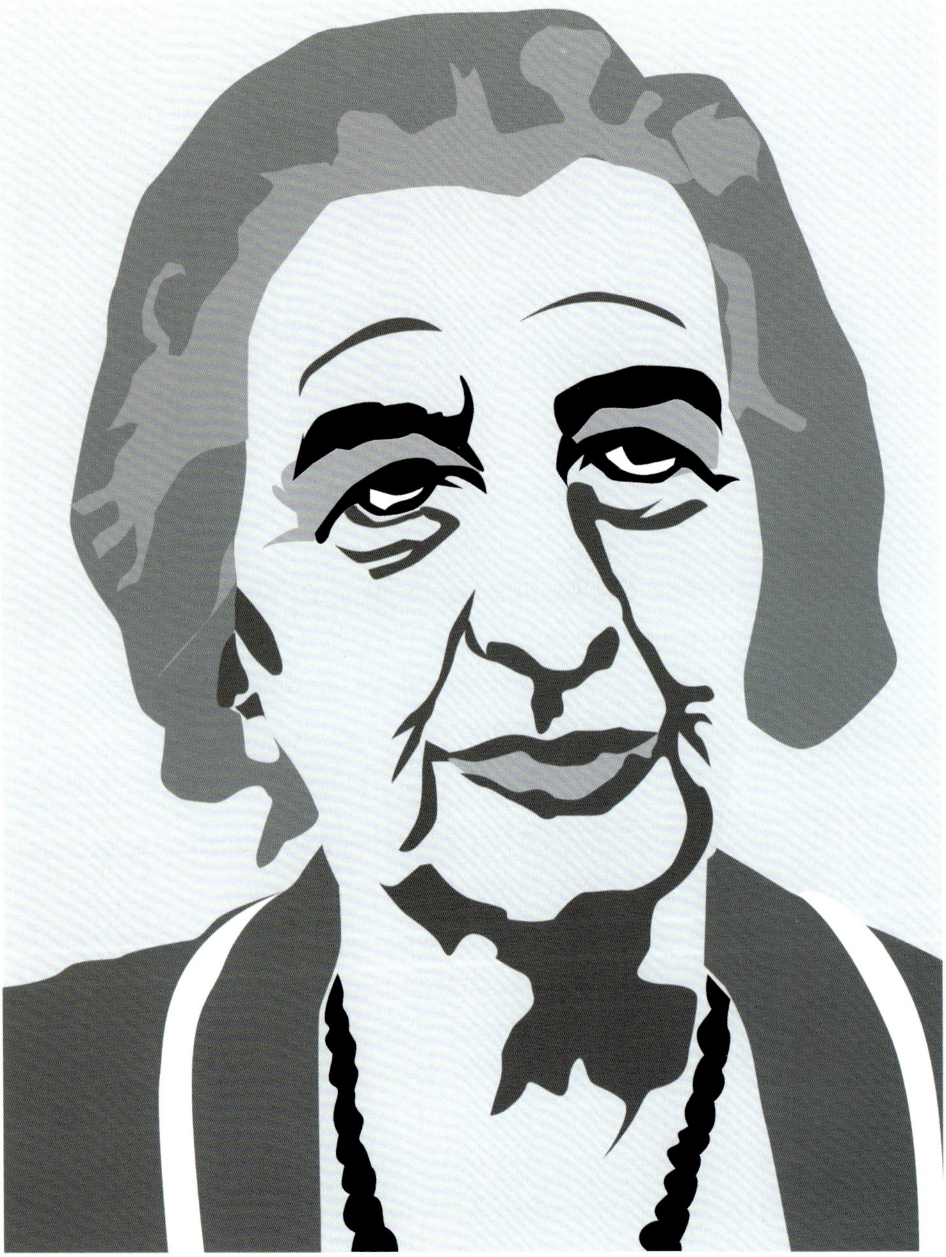

Golda Meir

spent the next decades working to bring other Jewish people to Palestine, serving as a manager of the construction arm of a trade union, and eventually becoming the head of the Jewish Agency's Political Department.

Much of Golda Meir's early work supported the settlement of Jewish people in Palestine and the creation of the Israeli state. Arab people already lived in these areas, but after more than six million Jews were killed in the ***Holocaust***, few in the international community wished to oppose creating a state for Jewish people. Golda Meir was a member of the provisional government responsible for the creation of the Israeli state. She also served as Israel's Ambassador to the Soviet Union, Minister of Labor and National Insurance, Foreign Minister, and ultimately as Prime Minister of Israel.

Golda Meir was only the third woman in the world to achieve the rank of Prime Minister, and she was seventy years old when she rose to this position! During her term, she continued to encourage Jewish settlement of Israel, worked to solidify Israeli relations with the United States, and attempted to negotiate peace with the surrounding states. On this last point, however, she was unsuccessful. In the final year of her leadership, Egypt and Syria, backed by nine other nations, invaded Israel. The invasion occurred on Yom Kippur, the holiest day of the Jewish calendar, and the following war became known as the Yom Kippur War. Golda Meir had always been a strong leader, and on the day of the attack, she encouraged her nation with these words:

> Citizens of Israel,
> This is not the first time that we have been compelled to endure ordeal by battle. I am confident that none among us will fall prey to panic. The mobilization will no doubt cause hardships and interference in the normal course of life and work but we must try to accept these difficultics as we have done in the past, with full understanding. We are called upon to demonstrate responsibility and discipline in our conduct. We must be ready for every burden and sacrifice needed for the defense of our survival, our freedom and our independence. Let us, then, conduct ourselves

> so as to be worthy of our soldiers of Israel who are valiantly doing their duty in the air, in the armoured forces, on the ships, in the artillery, in all units and services in the outposts, in the villages and settlements, along the lines of fire in all sectors.

Israel was eventually victorious in driving back the invading armies, but the war was ultimately seen as evidence of failures in Israel's leadership and diplomacy. After the war, Golda Meir was elected to another term as prime minister, but she resigned soon after the election. Nevertheless, to this day she continues to be remembered as a strong leader of her people and a great Jewish woman.

NAWAL EL SAADAWI

Born in 1931 in a small Egyptian village, it may have seemed that there was little hope for this girl to one day be anything but a traditional wife and mother. She was one of nine children in a land where few girls received education or opportunities. But Nawal El Saadawi would defy many people and traditions in her quest for equality and truth. This quest would land her in jail and threaten her life, but it would also turn the world's eyes to the plight of Arab women.

One of Nawal El Saadawi's first great accomplishments was receiving an education. She became a psychiatrist and was eventually appointed to a government position as Egypt's Director of Public Health. In this role, Saadawi had already achieved much more than most Egyptian women of the time could dream, but she wasn't about to sit quietly and thank the Egyptian government for its kindness. Instead, she opened her eyes to the many contradictions, oppressions, and hypocrisies around her and began to speak out about women's powerless position in Egyptian and Arab society.

Since Saadawi's background was in science and medicine, her first works concerning women focused on these subjects. In 1972, she published *Women and Sex*. This book was extremely controversial, and many ***conservative*** people

NAWAL AL MOUTAOUAKIL

In the 1984 Los Angeles Olympics, Nawal al Moutaouakil became the first Moroccan and the first woman from a Muslim country to ever take gold. She made her achievement in the four-hundred-meter hurdles. Today, she serves in the Moroccan government as a Junior Minister of Social Affairs in the division of youth and sport.

were enraged that this woman would dare to openly challenge notions about women's sexuality, politics, and religion. There were those who supported Saadawi, seeing her as a revolutionary and hoping her writings would be a ***catalyst*** for change, but the Egyptian government now saw her as a danger to the state. She was stripped of her position in the government, as editor of a health magazine, and as a board member of the Medical Association of Egypt.

These, however, would not be the biggest challenges Saadawi would face. She continued to write books about women's oppression, tackling subjects like ***female genital mutilation***, domestic violence, and Islamic fundamentalism. By 1980, the Egyptian government had enough of Saadawi's agitating and criticisms. She was imprisoned, a punishment that was meant to silence her, but that would only more firmly cement Saadawi's beliefs and determination.

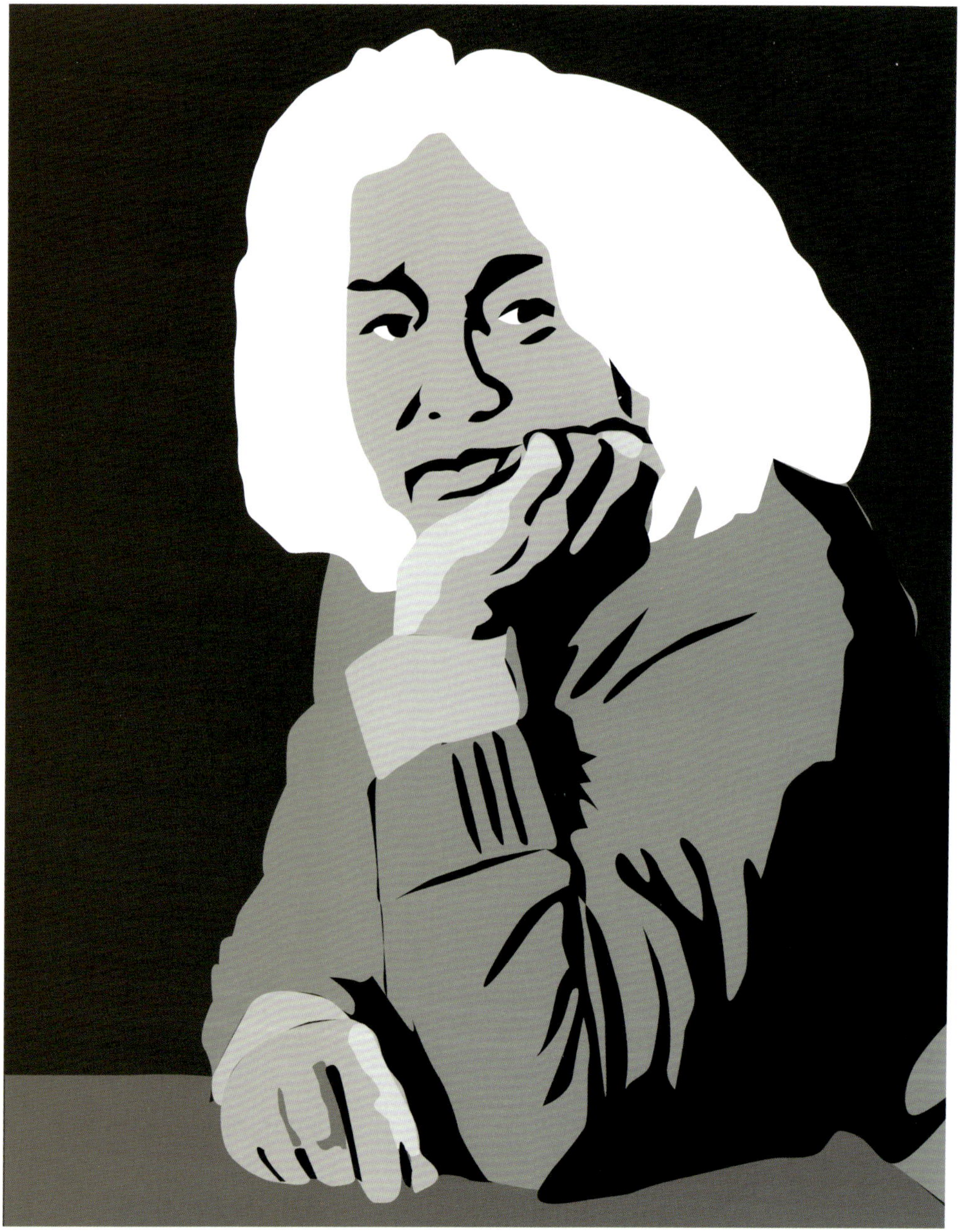

Nawal El Saadawi

With a change in the Egyptian leadership, Saadawi was released from prison. She began a women's organization that was soon, like her writings, banned. She continued to write, winning both awards and death threats. Today, Nawal El Saadawi's work continues uninterrupted. Though she has been forced to live behind armed guards and fanatical organizations have issued her "death warrant," Saadawi continues to believe in and work for women's liberation in the Mediterranean and around the world.

In one of Nawal El Saadawi's books she states, "Danger has been a part of my life ever since I picked up a pen and wrote. Nothing is more perilous than truth in a world that lies. Nothing is more perilous than knowledge in a world that has considered knowledge a sin since Adam and Eve." Indeed, many women throughout Mediterranean history have struggled in the quest for truth, knowledge, and equality, meeting both persecution and success along the way. Some have lived quiet lives while others have achieved greatness. All have contributed to their communities and our world.

Of course we do not have time here to review all the amazing women who have ever lived in and influenced the Mediterranean region, but from just these few examples, you can see that women play a vital role in their communities and in the world. Throughout history and even today, women's work and influence has gone unrecognized or been underappreciated, but this does not diminish women's abilities or importance. In the Mediterranean, women have been wives, mothers, business women, leaders, warriors, saints, artists, scientists, authors, and every other occupation known to humankind. Their proud legacy lives on in the Mediterranean women of today. Buoyed by new opportunities in education, employment, and government, their strength and contributions will continue to increase tomorrow.

FURTHER READING

Blundell, Sue. *Women in Ancient Greece*. Cambridge, Mass.: Harvard University Press, 1995.

Boccaccio, Giovanni. *Famous Women*. Cambridge, Mass.: Harvard University Press, 2001.

Flint, David. *The Mediterranean and Its People*. New York: Thomson Learning, 1994.

Harik, Ramsay M. and Elsa Marston. *Women in the Middle East: Tradition and Change*. New York: Franklin Watts, Inc., 2003.

Leon, Vicki. *Outrageous Women of Ancient Times*. New York: Wiley and Sons, 1998.

MacDonald, Fiona. *Women in Medieval Times*. Lincolnwood, Ill.: Peter Bedrick Books, 2000.

Pomeroy, Sarah B. *Spartan Women*. Oxford, New York: Oxford University Press, 2002.

Rolka, Gail Meyer. *100 Women Who Shaped World History*. San Francisco, Calif.: Bluewood Books, 1994.

Saadawi, Nawal El. *Walking Through Fire: A Life of Nawal El Saadawi*. New York: Zed Books Ltd., 2002.

Watterson, Barbara. *Women in Ancient Egypt*. New York: St. Martin's Press, 1991.

FOR MORE INFORMATION

Distinguished Women of Past and Present
www.distinguishedwomen.com

Individual country information from the CIA's *The World Factbook*
www.cia.gov/cia/publications/factbook/index.html

"The First Christians"
www.pbs.org/wgbh/pages/frontline/shows/religion/first/women.html

Islam 101.com: Women
www.islam101.com/women

Joan of Arc Online Archive
archive.joan-of-arc.org

Judaism 101: The Role of Women
www.jewfaq.org/women.htm

Nawal El Saadawi and Sherif Hetata Website
www.nawalsaadawi.net

United Nations Women Watch: Country Specific Information about Women Around the World
www.un.org/womenwatch

Women in the Ancient World
www.womenintheancientworld.com

Women Who Lead: A Project of the Sophia Foundation
www.womenwholead.org

Publisher's note:
The Web sites listed on these pages were active at the time of publication. The publisher is not responsible for Web sites that have changed their addresses or discontinued operation since the date of publication. The publisher will review and update the Web sites upon each reprint.

GLOSSARY

architectural Relating to the art or science of building.

aristocrat A member of nobility.

canonized Declared someone who is dead a saint.

catalyst Something that sparks or speeds up significant change or action.

civil Relating to citizens and their relationships with their government.

colonial Relating to a territory that has ties with a parent country.

conquistadors Sixteenth-century Spanish conquerors of Mexico, Peru, and America.

conservative Tending to follow existing views, conditions, or institutions.

coveted Enviously desired or wished for.

degradation Declined to a low, poor, or demoralized state.

destabilized Caused a government to become unable to function or survive.

domestic Relating to the household and the family.

ethnic Relating to groups of people classed by common racial, national, tribal, religious, linguistic, or cultural origin or background.

ethnic cleansing The killing, driving out, or imprisonment or ethnic minorities by a dominant majority group.

female genital mutilation Term used to refer to the removal of part, or all, of the female genitalia.

fundamentalist A religious believer who stresses strict and literal obedience to the religion's principles.

gender The traits (behavioral, cultural, or psychological) associated with one sex.

genocide The purposeful, systematic destruction of a racial, political, or cultural group.

heretic Someone who disagrees with traditional church doctrines or beliefs.

Holocaust The mass slaughter of European civilians, especially Jews, by the Nazis during World War II.

indelible Unforgettable; making marks that cannot be erased, removed, or washed away.

individualistic Pursuing an independent course of thought or action.

infamous Having the worst kind or reputation.

infant mortality The number of infants who die within the first year of life in relation to number of live births.

infiltrated Passed into something by diffusing or permeating through it.

infrastructure A system's underlying foundation or basic framework.

lineage Descent in a line from a common ancestor.

literacy The ability to read and write.

nomadic Relating to people without fixed residency, who move seasonally from place to place within a particular territory.

opaque Blocking passage of radiant energy, especially light.

Palestinian A person of Arab descent living in the West Bank of Israel; this region has had limited self-rule since 1993.

per capita Equally to every individual.

polarizing Breaking up into opposing groups.

Qur'an The book containing the sacred writings Muslims accept as revelations made to Muhammad by Allah through the angel Gabriel.

regent Someone who governs a kingdom for a minor, disabled, or absent sovereign.

rogue Isolated and destructive.

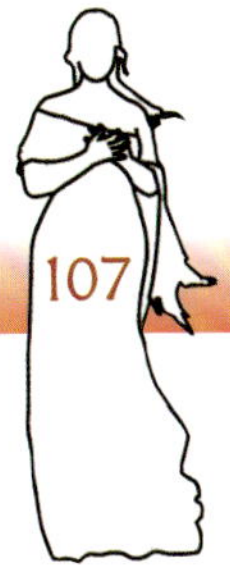

secular Relating to the worldly; not overtly religious.

self-determination Free choice of one's acts without external influence.

socioeconomic status Relating to the state of one's social and economic position in society.

start-up capital The initial money raised to set a venture in motion.

statistics A branch of mathematics that deals with collection, analysis, interpretation, and presentation of masses of numerical data.

stereotypes Standardized mental pictures held in common by a group representing an oversimplified opinion or prejudiced attitude.

subservient Subordinate; submissive.

Suez Canal A canal in northeast Egypt that crosses the Isthmus of Suez, between the Mediterranean and Red seas, connecting Africa and Asia.

Torah The wisdom and law of Jewish scripture and other sacred writings and oral traditions.

transgressions Violations of a command or law.

triumvirate A ruling body or commission of three people.

urbanization The process of becoming more like a city.

Western Relating to the noncommunist countries of Europe and America.

winnowing Removing by a current of air.

INDEX

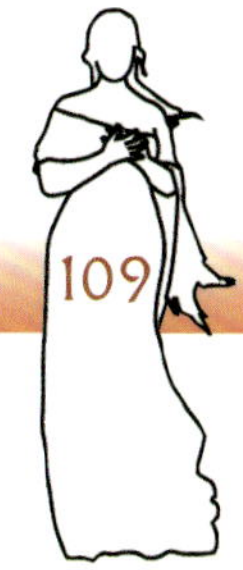

PICTURE CREDITS

Cover: Studio1, Benjamin Stewart, Stockbyte, Corel
Author's Image: pp. 12, 18, 21, 22, 25, 26, 28, 32, 59, 60, 70
Benjamin Stewart: pp. 57, 64, 77, 92
Corel: pp. 35, 41, 43, 44, 46, 82
Digital Stock: pp. 38, 51, 54, 63, 69, 73, 78, 89

BIOGRAPHIES

Autumn Libal is a freelance author and illustrator living in Vancouver, British Columbia. She received her degree from Smith College, an all women's college in Northampton, Massachusetts, where she developed a deep interest in women's issues. Autumn's writing has also appeared in *New Moon: The Magazine for Girls and Their Dreams,* as well as other Mason Crest series including, NORTH AMERICAN FOLKLORE and NORTH AMERICAN INDIANS TODAY.

Dr. Mary Jo Dudley is the director of Cornell University's Gender and Global Change Department, which focuses on the evolving role of gender around the world. She is also the associate director of Latin American Studies at Cornell.